TUDOR AND STUART DRAWINGS

Under the editorship of
K. T. Parker

*

THE DRAWINGS OF HENRY FUSELI
by Nicolas Powell

THE DRAWINGS OF RICHARD WILSON
by Brinsley Ford

THE DRAWINGS OF FRANCESCO GUARDI
by J. Byam Shaw

TUDOR AND STUART DRAWINGS
by John Woodward

John Woodward

TUDOR
AND
STUART
DRAWINGS

FABER AND FABER

24 Russell Square

London

First published in mcmli
by Faber and Faber Limited
24 Russell Square London W.C.1
Printed in Great Britain by
R. MacLehose and Company Limited
The University Press Glasgow

CONTENTS

PREFACE   *page* 9

INTRODUCTION   11

CATALOGUE OF PLATES   43

INDEX   55

PLATES   *after page* 59

7

PREFACE

Perhaps the most desirable contribution to a study of drawings produced in England during the time of the Tudor and Stuart dynasties, would be a large, liberally illustrated, dictionary of the artists whom it has been possible to identify. This book cannot claim to be, in any way, so ambitious and serves only as a brief introduction to a collection of plates, at least half of which have never before been published.

Artists from this period, who have already been studied at some length, have been represented but slightly in comparison to their worth. This is particularly so in the case of Inigo Jones, and the topographers, Hollar and Place. More prominence than usual has been given to the portrait draughtsmen, except in the medium of pastel and plumbago. The work of Sir Peter Lely has especially seemed in need of a complete revaluation: that of Holbein, Van Dyck and the Van de Veldes has been excluded for obvious reasons.

This study of the drawings of the seventeenth century owes a great debt to the organisers of the Exhibitions of the *Works of British-Born Artists of the Seventeenth Century,* held at the Burlington Fine Arts Club in 1938, and of *Seventeenth Century Art in Europe* at Burlington House in the same year. The catalogues of these exhibitions are full of information, and have been invaluable in locating drawings.

I should like to thank Dr K. T. Parker, who first suggested that I should undertake this work, for his help with the text and for his assistance in the final selection of the plates; Mr E. K. Waterhouse, who not only lent me photographs, but has answered patiently the many questions I have put to him; Sir Henry Hake for advice on the Holbeinesque tracings; Professor J. G. Van Gelder for the loan of photographs; Mr Edward Croft Murray for his help over the drawings in the British Museum; Mr Oliver Millar, who is himself engaged on a biography of Lely; and Sir Robert Witt, for permission to consult his library.

It is a pleasure to acknowledge the kindness of the many private collectors and museum officials who have allowed me to examine and reproduce drawings, and at the same time have given me advice and information.

I am grateful for the help of Mr Richard Brett-Smith and of Mr Nicolas Powell, who kindly read and corrected my manuscript.

July 1949

J. O. W.

INTRODUCTION

The Tudors and the new class they created had little use for an artist's services. Their huge palaces and houses were not filled with paintings, and the work they had to offer was of a more utilitarian and ephemeral nature—the painting of shields and pennants for tournaments, and the decoration of triumphal arches. Even the demand for portraits, which was to monopolise the artist in the next century, was limited to dynastic occasions and to propaganda. The private picture gallery was not to develop until the next century, and a portrait was invariably painted to give away. The monarch was shown as the personification of power and magnificence to impress neighbouring states, and the artist was essential to him in the more personal, though none the less political, matter of bride-choosing.

Holbein at first had to content himself with the patronage of the German merchants of the Steelyard; it was not until later that he found Court patronage and its ensuing demands on his skill. He brought in a more personal approach to painting, however, with his development of the miniature.

Knowledge of the arts in England during the sixteenth century is still very limited; although much information has perished for ever, it is possible that more may be found in manuscript sources, and a little intense research may reveal new facts concerning the Sergeant painters, who worked during the time of Holbein and immediately after his death. Only in 1861 was it discovered that Holbein died eleven years earlier than had been imagined. If this fact lay buried so long it is hardly surprising that information concerning lesser artists has still not been excavated.

There are few surviving drawings from this period, and nearly all of them present special problems. It is the famous collection of Holbein drawings at Windsor that must be the starting point for any study of Tudor draughtsmen. These portrait drawings were not made for the sitter's retention, unlike those produced by Clouet in France, but were merely part of the working material towards the finished portrait or miniature. Although there is no proof, it is reasonable to presume that these drawings were still in Holbein's studio at Whitehall when he suddenly died of the plague in 1543. The immediate use to which the studio was put is not known, though at a later date it became an archive room, and it is probable that these drawings escaped destruction on account of their completeness and iconographic interest. It may be that this was also the reason for the preservation of the Chatsworth cartoon of Henry

VII and Henry VIII. Conjecture apart, the book would appear to have been in the possession of Edward VI, for the first unimpeachable reference to it appears in the Lumley inventory of 1590[1]: 'A greate Booke of Pictures doone by Hannce Holbein of certyn lordes, ladyes, gentlemen and gentlewomen of King Henry the 8 his tyme ... which book was King Edward 6.' In the same inventory is the Chatsworth cartoon. Somewhere on its subsequent journeys the book not only probably shed some of the drawings it contained, but appears, in addition, to have gathered four drawings, not by Holbein himself, which are preserved with the rest in the Royal Library. One of these, representing *Henry Howard, Earl of Surrey,* (Pl. 3) is probably English, while of the others one has already been attributed, it would appear rightly, to some French artist, and the other two are so overworked that it would be impossible to make any conjecture concerning them, except to say that they were not by Holbein.

This drawing of the *Earl of Surrey,* wrongly inscribed with the name of his father, seems to have very definite affiliations with another of the same sitter, now correctly inscribed, in the Morgan Library (Pl. 2). The latter was also once in the great book: it is known, in fact, to have hung in Queen Caroline's closet at Kensington. From the diagram of this room by Vertue,[2] it can be seen that three drawings that hung there then are no longer in the Royal Collection. One is described as a profile drawing of Surrey, and certainly the Morgan drawing bears the familiar Roman lettering; closer examination shows, moreover, that the 'Hen' of *Henry Howard* is an emendation of 'Tho'.[3]

Both drawings have considerable merit and style, though below the Holbein standard. They are certainly English, done either in the studio or by some pupil, a fact not without interest, as Holbein was in England for a little under ten years, and appears to have left no school or following, nor, for that matter, any real influence, except on miniature painters such as Hilliard. It is not even known what exactly there was to influence. Certainly English painting, until well into the next century, displays a tradition gathered from mediaeval craftsmen via the large portrait-painting workshops, and not from Holbein.

Assuming, therefore, that we have two English drawings among the Holbein collection, it becomes of great importance to see how they came to be there. Either they were added by one of the book's less discerning owners as genuine Holbeins, or they were merely collected because they were of the Earl of Surrey, of whom there are two genuine Holbeins in the collection. This suggestion would apply especially to the Earl of Arundel, or his family, as Surrey was his great-grandfather. That Arundel was proud of this ancestor can be gauged from the fact that his portrait, similar to

[1] *Walpole Society,* vol. VI, p. 27.

[2] *A Catalogue of the Pictures etc. belonging to James II, to which is added a Catalogue of the pictures and drawings in the Cabinet of the late Queen Caroline.* Bathoe, 1758.

[3] Parker: *Drawings of Hans Holbein at Windsor Castle,* London, 1945, p. 20 and note 7.

(Pl. 3), though this could not have served as a study for it, can be seen on the wall in Philip Fruytiers' painting (after Van Dyck) of the Earl and Countess.[1] A so far unnoticed hint of the addition of spurious Holbeins appears in Edward Norgate's book on *Limning*.[2] He says 'of this kinde was an excellent booke while it remained in the hands of the most noble Earl of Arundel and Surrey. But I heare it has been a great traveller, and wherever now, he hath got his errata'. This sentence, in its context, refers to the wanderings of the book both after and before it came into the hands of Arundel, and uses the word 'errata' strangely. There is probably a pun on the Latin verb *Erro,* from which it is derived, and implies an addition of a few non-Holbein items. Norgate has confused his meaning, but this would appear to be the only explanation to account for the presence of (Pl. 2) and (3) in the book at a comparatively early time.

Round these two Surrey drawings it is possible to build up a small collection of similar drawings, which are sometimes labelled as by Holbein or his School, and are known to have been done in this country. These include the *Unknown Man* at the Victoria and Albert Museum and the head of *Henry VIII* at Munich, and almost certainly the *Sir Charles Wingfield* in the Boymans, which is a copy of the Windsor version.[3] These drawings are all manifestly of a weaker execution than Holbein's, though of some quality, and it is only recently that the Munich one has been doubted. In addition, they are all the work of a right-handed draughtsman which is sufficient, on the evidence of the Windsor drawings, to disqualify Holbein. They are all, almost certainly, by an English hand.

A further series of Holbeinesque drawings was sold in 1937 and broken up, partly between the National Portrait Gallery and private collectors.[4] The items from this portfolio are puzzling, and a great deal more of the workings of the portrait factories needs to be known before we can accurately gauge their use. They range from drawings of people contemporary with the Holbein series to one of George Talbot, 6th Earl of Shrewsbury, dated 1580. This would suggest, by the mere fact that they cover so lengthy a period and yet have remained together, that they were not the gleanings from a painter's studio, but actual patterns from a factory which turned out duplicate portraits for cadet branches of families or for institutions. Most of them have been silhouetted, and while some are in chalk, others are on transparent oil paper which would suggest, as they are not good enough to be Holbein's own tracings from the life on the apparatus he may have used, that they were taken from original work and used as mere duplicating machinery. If that is so, they are some of the few survivals from this factory system that can give any idea of its organisation.

[1] Mary Hervey: *Earl of Arundel,* reproduced page 434.
[2] Final version of 1648/50—Bodleian Library, MS. Tanner 326.   [3] Parker: *op. cit.,* p. 46, repr.
[4] C. F. Bell: *Burlington Magazine,* vol. LXXXVII (1945) p. 189. For a discussion on the provenance of these drawings see Catalogue entry for Plate 4.

Though all this must be conjecture, it would seem certain that they are not later than the sixteenth century. They are not beautiful drawings: only the *Bishop Fisher* (Plate IV) shows any marked degree of sensitivity, possibly because the tracer had a better model to work from.

Holbein's influence did not outlast his death, and his place was taken by artists of meagre talent from the Low Countries, of whom little is known beyond their names. Portrait drawings are unknown until the revival of miniature painting by Hilliard and Oliver. There is, however, one exception, a portrait of *Thomas Howard 4th Duke of Norfolk,* which was once in the collection of Arundel, and which is by Lucas de Here (1534–84), an artist of whom little is known.[1] Many of the works formerly ascribed to him were found to be by Hans Eworth. This drawing could equally well, on considerations of style, be given to this same earlier artist, if it were not for the fact that there is said to be a sixteenth-century ascription on the back to de Here.[2] This portrait, judging from reproductions, has all the appearance of being what it is claimed to be, and therefore makes an interesting link between Holbein and Hilliard. During the latter half of the century there is a little more material. Several distinguished artists visited this country, and have left behind valuable records. Anthonis Van Den Wyngaerde accompanied Philip of Spain to England for a visit to Mary Tudor and made drawings of the countryside between Dover and London.[3] The Flemish artist, Joris Hoefnagel (1541–1600), described by Carel Van Mander as 'a young, rich and learned man, travelled much, visiting many countries, and made a very big book of all interesting things which he found and saw,' came here some time between 1568 and 1570, and left valuable records of Windsor, Nonesuch, and Oxford.[4] The most interesting visitor, however, was Frederigo Zuccaro, an Italian, who, during the reign of Elizabeth, was perhaps the most celebrated painter in Europe. He seems to have arrived in England at the end of 1574 and to have been back in Italy by October, 1575, so that the shortness of his visit is out of all proportion to the influence he is supposed to have had on English portraiture, quite apart from the number of paintings which are still given his name in English country houses. Two drawings in the British Museum are perfectly autographed; they represent *Queen Elizabeth* and the *Earl of Leicester,* and are both from the life and certainly among the most interesting survivals from this period.[5]

Fortunately, there are two surviving drawings by the one considerable English

[1] Hervey: *op. cit.,* reproduced Plate 2.   [2] Williamson: *Connoisseur,* LIII (1919) p. 135.

[3] In the Sutherland collection in the Ashmolean. See E. Croft-Murray's Catalogue of an exhibition held in the British Museum 1949/50: *The Beginning of English Topographical and Landscape Drawing.*

[4] Puyvelde: *Flemish Drawings at Windsor Castle,* London, 1942. p. 15.

[5] No painting corresponding to the Elizabeth is known, but Mr E. K. Waterhouse, *Burlington Magazine,* vol. LXIX (1936), p. 133 has suggested that the Italianate portrait of Leicester, formerly at Stafford House and now in America, may have had its foundation in the British Museum drawing. Both the Zuccaro drawings are reproduced in this article.

painter, Nicholas Hilliard. This artist was born in 1547, and died two years after Oliver in 1619, but, whereas he is almost wholly Elizabethan in feeling and technique, Oliver belongs entirely to the early seventeenth century. Hilliard is the first English artist of whom we have a reasonable knowledge, from over a hundred attributable miniatures and a document of the greatest importance, his *Art of Limning*.[1]

Hilliard was the son of a goldsmith at Exeter, and appears to have begun painting miniatures by 1560. Some time in the late seventies he was in France. Certainly in 1577 he was *valet de chambre* to the Duc d'Alençon, and his style was influenced by the current court fashions in painting and by the work of François Clouet. His style from then on was to combine the direct observation of Holbein with the easy grace of French mannerism. In England he became limner and goldsmith to the Queen and was continued in this office by James I.

The *Art of Limning* was written at the request of Richard Haydocke (who had already eulogised both Hilliard and his pupil, Isaac Oliver, in his translation of Lomazzo in 1598); it is a stylistically involved document which, none the less, sheds much light on his method of work, and underlines his debt to Holbein and Dürer. From this treatise it is fairly easy to follow his process of work from the laying of the parchment to the finished miniature. An excellent example of the technique can be seen in the exquisite, unfinished miniature of a lady in the collection of Mr Louis Clarke where his original pencil lines on the parchment can be seen quite clearly. Also in this treatise he mentions a black-and-white artist, who would otherwise be unknown to us. Talking of patronage, Hilliard remarks 'Neuertheless, if a man be so indued by nature and liue in time of trouble, and vnder a sauage gouerment wherin arts be not esteemed, and himself but of small meanes, woe be unto him as vnto an vntimly birth; for of mine owne knowlege it hath mad poure men poorer, as among others many, the most rare Englishe drawer of story works in black and white, John Bossam, for one of his skill worthy to haue been sergeant painter to any King or Emperour, whose work in that kind are comperable with the best whatsoeuer in cloathe in distemper cullors for whit and black; whoe being very poore, and belyke wanting to buy faier cullors, wrought therefore for the most part in whit and black, and growing yet poorer by charge of children etc. gaue painting cleane ouer, . . . only unfortunat becasse he was English borne, for euen the strangers would otherwisse haue set him vpp'. Nothing by Bossam is known to exist—he later became a minister—but this passage makes it clear that he worked in black and white only because he was too poor to afford colours, not because there was any particular demand for work of this kind.

The first of Hilliard's drawings (Pl. 6) is a graceful and delicate study of a *Lady*

[1] Published by the *Walpole Society*, vol. I, edited by Philip Norman. The transcription is not entirely accurate or complete.

in Court Dress, which is almost wholly French in feeling, and as a recent writer has suggested, 'the image is conceived as a geometrical abstraction devoid of volumetric significance.'[1] It is interesting to compare it with the freer and looser full-length of Elizabeth by Zuccaro, already mentioned. The second is the design, probably for the great seal of Ireland, which is so close in style to the great seal of England mentioned in Elizabeth's letter of September 15th 1584, that it would seem reasonable to date this drawing from the same time.

Hilliard, like Holbein, must have made studies, in pencil or chalk, from the life before painting his miniatures, although the *Art of Limning* would suggest the contrary; but nothing of the sort has ever come to light.[2] Nor was there a fashion, as in France, for crayon portraits. These had become popular under Francis I, and were still enthusiastically collected by Catherine de Medici, who could write to the governess of her children in June 1552: '*Ne fauldrez de faire paindre au vif par le painctre que vous avez par de là tous mes enfants, tant fils que filles, avec la roine d'Ecosse, sans rien oblier de leur visaiges, mais il suffist que ce soit au créon, pour avoir plus tost faict, et me les envoyez le plus tost que vous pourrez*'.[3] Catherine left behind at her death some five hundred crayon portraits of her family and her Court. If Elizabeth had left a similar collection, inscribed with the names of courtiers, countless iconographical problems would solve themselves, especially the tantalising anonymity of so many of Hilliard's miniatures. Drawings of this nature from France were certainly circulating in England in the closing days of the century, but were not to be a popular English practice till the middle of the next century.

The other Englishman whose work has come down to us is John White; in his way typical of his age—half pirate, half artist—he worked between 1585 and 1593.[4] He has some right to be considered the first English water-colour painter, with technical attributes that are usually connected with the eighteenth-century practitioners. White was not only a painter, but also a colonial pioneer, and made no less than five voyages to Virginia (now North Carolina), where he was the first governor. His daughter, indeed, appears to have been the mother of the first English child to be born in North America. He was a skilful and observant man, and made sketches, both in his colony and on his voyages, which are now preserved in the British Museum. Customs and costumes, animals and birds, were meticulously sketched in water colour, sometimes with pen outlines; and he appears to have encountered on his voyages Esquimaux and natives of the Caucasus and Astrakhan, as well as the Virginians. Not content

[1] John Pope-Hennessy, *A Lecture on Nicholas Hilliard,* London, 1949, p. 26.
[2] Miss Erna Auerbach in an article, *More Light on Hilliard, Burlington Magazine,* vol. XCI, 1949, p. 167, draws attention to a 'book of portraitures' which Hilliard had in his hands in 1570–1. This may refer to drawings by himself rather than to engravings or illuminations.
[3] Jean Leymarie, *Les Crayons Français du XVIe Siècle,* Paris, 1947.
[4] L. Binyon, *Walpole Society,* vol. XIII, where many of his drawings are reproduced.

with the people he saw, he conjured from his evidently very vivid imagination a number of drawings of Ancient Britons. De Bry published these, together with twenty-three Virginia drawings, in his *America* (1590) '*ad demonstrandum, Britanniae incolas non minus liquando fuisse sylvestres ipsis Virginiensibus*'.

The only other drawings that can be connected with Englishmen are decorative, such as the illustrations to the Lumley Inventory itself, which are rich and ornate, and make it an unusually beautiful document. These motifs are descended from the old illuminated manuscript workers, revived by the miniature. Initial letters of official proclamations and documents, with the minutely painted head of the sovereign, continue this craft into the eighteenth century.[1]

After the Reformation direct contact with Italy was broken, and her influence was only manifest in the Protestant refugees, who had absorbed her culture into their own idiom. These men from the Low Countries were able to overcome the short-lived French influence, which had succeeded the breach with Rome, and to dominate the English scene. The seventeenth century opened quietly and with no immediate signs of change; James I was content to sit to Van Somer and Mytens for his official likeness, while, across the channel, Louis XIII was to patronise Champaigne and Peter Paul Rubens, the great protégé of the Archduchess Isabella. In the 1620's Philip IV was to have the first of that wonderful series of portraits from the brush of Velasquez; and amidst all this activity in Court painting Rembrandt was to produce in the 30's the first of his matchless series of self-portraits.

Travel and a new connoisseurship brought in a change of taste, a wave of patronage and collecting. The credit for this belongs in the first place to the Earl of Arundel and to Henry, Prince of Wales, and later to Charles I, the greatest collector and connoisseur of them all, and to the Duke of Buckingham.

The story of the collecting of paintings and drawings by Englishmen in the seventeenth century merits a separate study. Not only did it mean that Whitehall became a great picture gallery, but Charles also persuaded such celebrated artists as Rubens and Van Dyck to work for him. For the English painter there were two advantages: he could study and copy the work of the great masters, if given access to the collections, and he could profit by observing or assisting such a man as Van Dyck. For his own work there was little demand, though a few artists, such as Dobson and Walker, both Englishmen, emerged as considerable figures of the period immediately before and after Van Dyck's death. They might have broken down the old workshop traditions, but many Englishmen from lack of patronage had to be content to serve in the studios of the visitors. None the less an art which had hardly

---

1 Much sixteenth-century topography was no more than beautifully drawn and coloured cartography. For this reason, the work of John Norden (1548/1625), John Thomas and Vincent Volpe is not discussed here. There is a useful article on Volpe by Miss Erna Auerbach in *Burlington Magazine,* Vol. XCII, 1950, p. 222.

even been apparent—unlike music, architecture, landscape gardening, and above all, literature—began quite obviously to take shape.

There is now much more material, almost an abundance of it, to enable a study to be made of drawings during the years covered by the combined reigns of the House of Stuart. Even this richness is poor in comparison with the survivals from other European countries. Though the collection of old master and contemporary drawings was a great vogue—and none were keener collectors than the painters—it seems to have been taken for granted that there were few drawings in England worthy of retention. It would be wrong to pretend that the English drawings of this period are of the highest sensitivity and quality when compared with those of other acknowledged European masters; but it is just as ridiculous to reject them off-hand, and very little attention has ever been paid to them. A further study is rewarding, and makes a light background commentary on this politically turbulent century.

The drawings themselves fall into four main categories: (1) *Architectural drawings* from men such as Webb, Wren, and Jones, who stand outside this book; (2) those which may perhaps be termed *Drawings of Fancy*—the work mainly of Inigo Jones and Isaac Oliver; (3) *Landscape and topographical drawings*; (4) *Portrait drawings,* which form by far the largest section, as well as the least studied. It will, perhaps, make both for coherence and usefulness if they are considered under those headings rather than chronologically.

Isaac Oliver was a prolific draughtsman, and his drawings, in any assessment, must take second place to his superb miniatures, for they vary both in skill and in style; obviously many of them are merely hurried jottings on leaves, since detached, of sketch-books. Vertue mentions two such: '*Severall leaves of Tabletts belonging to bookes of I. Oliver that he carried in his pocket to sketch in with a silver penn*' and '*a vellum pocket book that was I. Olivers and therein are many sketches, postures, etc., done with a silver pen by himself and in several leaves the remains of writing*'. Other drawings are large set-pieces which demonstrate his receptiveness to the style of other artists, though his skill, like that of Inigo Jones, raises the composition from mere pastiche to originality.

Oliver, who was born before 1568, came from Rouen to England with his father in order to escape the Catholic persecutions. He learned the art of miniature painting from Hilliard whose rival he eventually became, though, in fact, their methods of approach were entirely different. Oliver preferred the round and decorative treatment of his subject, as opposed to the flattened and stylized image beloved by Hilliard.

In his drawings Oliver is various, though it is never hard to recognize his nervous and scratchy line. Sometimes he is reminiscent of the heavier northern style of Golzius and Moreelse and at others he seems perfectly at home in the mannered and rarefied atmosphere of Fontainebleau. But the most apparent influence is that of the Parmese artist, Parmigianino who developed under the influence of Correggio.

Sometimes Oliver is content with an almost straightforward pastiche, but more often prefers to combine the spirit of masquerade at the Jacobean Court with the formula of the other artist. The effect is nearly always elegant, but depends too much on linear qualities, and is without any great depth. Oliver may himself have acquired drawings by Parmigianino on his travels abroad but in any case he would probably have had access to the Earl of Arundel's cabinet of drawings. Arundel is known, from documents and engravings, to have been an eager collector of Parmigianino's works. He had made two journeys abroad; on one, of 1613–14 (before Oliver died), he was accompanied by Inigo Jones, and probably brought back originals by this draughtsman. One thing is certain—that Oliver must have known actual examples of these drawings, and not only engravings. Of his own travels abroad little is known. He was certainly in Venice in 1596, and may have been out of England in 1588.[1] It was in Venice that he came into contact with Rottenhammer, who, together with Elsheimer and Brill, was there introducing the small narrative cabinet painting. Oliver had an ambition to experiment with the same idea in England, and although some of his smaller miniatures in this vein, such as the *Diana* and the *Prodigal Son*, are by no means failures, his lamentable *Head of Christ* is an example of the danger of mere plagiarism. The large limning of the *Entombment*, which was completed by his son and was once in the collection of Charles I, has now disappeared. Ample information as to its appearance is to be found both in Vandendoort's inventory, and in the large drawing for it, (Pl. 11), which shows the strange combination of influences that make up his distinctive style.

The one surviving portrait drawing (Pl. 9) by Oliver is of such power and grace that it is much to be regretted, as in the case of Hilliard, that more of this kind has not survived. This *Head of a Young Boy* must be one of the most charming portrait heads by any artist working in England during the seventeenth century. There is in the Fitzwilliam Museum a *Self Portrait* drawing of Oliver's, which has suffered heavily, though it was obviously once of quality. Also in the Fitzwilliam is the slight and niggling drawing called *Lucy Harrington, Countess of Bedford,* which undoubtedly connects with the miniature in the same Museum; but it can only have served as a study for pose and costume, and was certainly not taken from life. There is an interesting pencil tracing in the Victoria and Albert Museum, a profile of *Anne of Denmark*,[2] from the miniature belonging to H.M. the King. This tracing was probably used to facilitate the manufacture of duplicate miniatures; but apart from these two studies there is no other drawing which can be connected with an Oliver portrait miniature.

Isaac Oliver bequeathed '*All my drawings already finished and unfinished and limned*

---

[1] G. Reynolds: *Hilliard and Oliver,* London 1947, p. 11.
[2] This and the *Lucy Harrington* are both reproduced by Reynolds *op. cit.*

pictures, be they histories, stories or anything of limning, whatsoever of my own handwork as yet unfinished . . . to my eldest son Peter, if he shall live and exercise that art or science which he and I now do.' Peter Oliver certainly did work with his father, and their style is probably so close that an injustice may be done to the son by assigning to him only a few drawings of weak character. Certainly the example reproduced here (Pl. 31) shows a more mannered and ungraceful use of the Parmegianinesque formula. Peter is too shadowy a figure to assess or disentangle as yet. He may, as Vertue suggests, have designed costumes for masques, and there is evidence that he is responsible for some of the figures in Barlow's drawings. He found his chief employment in making excellent miniature copies of the paintings in Charles I's collection, many of which survive, much in the same way as Teniers made his reduced copies of paintings belonging to the Archduke Leopold William.

Inigo Jones is perhaps the best known English artist of the period, and his architectural drawings and designs for masques have been frequently illustrated and discussed.[1] He is one of the most fascinating figures of his time and a true child of the new patronage that had grown up in England. While travelling in Italy he absorbed much of the culture of the Mediterranean, and his architecture and his drawings reflect his study and appreciation of Italian artists. He became an acknowledged authority at Court on the appraisal of works of art: an amusing description of him in this role still exists, and it is interesting to find that, in spite of his devotion to Italy, he remained at heart *'Puritanissimo Fiero'.*[2]

The masque 'developed as a brilliant spectacle at the Court of Elizabeth, but that stern economist gave it no undue encouragement. The two succeeding queens, Anne of Denmark and Henrietta Maria, patronised it even to recklessness, and poets, artists, and musicians seemed to spring up at their call . . . Ben Jonson gave it unity of design and coherent form; Inigo Jones made it a spectacle of beauty.'[3] The designs for some of the scenery and costumes for these entertainments are still preserved at Chatsworth, and are a contrast, in their airiness and charm, to the heavy clothes, furniture, and theological thinking which characterize the reign of James I. The Masque was the perfect plaything for the civilized Court of the second Stuart, and Inigo Jones was its great designer. At first Jonson and Jones worked well together, but at a later stage Jonson turned against his collaborator. He probably found that clothes and scenery tended to overshadow his words. The ladies of the Court infinitely preferred dressing up to learning their lines, and appreciating the beauty of them. Jonson seems only too aware of this when he writes:

> *Painting and carpentry are the soul of masque.*
> *Pack with your peddling poetry to the stage.*

[1] Simpson and Bell, *Walpole Society,* vol. XII, A. Nicoll, *Stuart Masques,* London 1937.
[2] R. Wittkower, *Burlington Magazine,* vol. XC (1948), p. 49.   [3] Simpson and Bell, *op. cit.,* p. 1.

The designs of Inigo Jones are, as would be expected, heavily influenced by his Italian contemporaries. The influence of Guercino, whom he met on his travels, is perhaps the most noticeable. There is in fact at Chatsworth a drawing of Guercino by Jones, who was seventeen years his senior. In the British Museum, the Ashmolean Museum, and elsewhere are sketches of heads—often many crowded together—which also mirror this fruitful acquaintance.

The fantasies of his sets and tableaux are rich in borrowings both from classical and baroque motifs, which accompany tropical palm trees and mysterious caverns, the whole displaying a lightness of touch and variation of invention which distinguished the creative artist from the heavy-handed plagiarist. He had studied the Tuscan theatre and the work of its designers, and the influence of Alfonso and Giulio Parigi is much in evidence in the costume designs, though none appear to be exact copies. In 1638 he designed the remarkable moonlight scenes for a masque attributed to Davenant, *Luminalia* (Pl. 17), which at about the same time were closely paralleled by Bernini's sets for *La Marina*. Is it too far-fetched to believe that Inigo Jones had in mind for this scene the painting by Adam Elsheimer, dated 1609, of the *Flight into Egypt*, with its haunting and beautiful reflected moonlight?[1] This picture could have been known to him from an engraving, and shows once again how, with an expert knowledge of the lighting and machinery of the stage, he could turn such a felicitous and unexpected piece of borrowing to his own uses. That Palladio, Parigi, and Guercino could influence so beneficially a puritan artist in the first half of the seventeenth century, is evidence of the remarkable change that travel and patronage had worked on English artists since the early days of workshop subservience. That this influence, except on such artists as Dobson, did not flourish, but lay dormant for nearly another century, is one of the tragedies of the history of English art. The blame for this did not rest entirely in the Civil War upheavals which were to come; rather did this Italian learning hold the seeds of its own dissolution. The patronage of renowned artists from abroad, such as Van Dyck and the Gentileschi, turned back the clock, and the momentum gathered by the native artist died down dispirited. No work was found for the English painter, except in a few isolated cases, such was the reputation of the man 'from abroad'. Flemish, Dutch, German and Swedish names dominate English paining from the Restoration to the advent of Thornhill. The English architects fell into no such disrepute, and what were for painters years of oblivion were glorious for them. The belief that an Englishman was builder, craftsman, and handyman, but not artist, took a long time to die. For all his learning and faultless taste it is not improbable that Jones was more appreciated for his ability to bring a masque to life (in much the same way as a sixteenth-century artist had

---

[1] Saxl and Wittkower, *English Art and the Mediterranean*, Oxford 1948, p. 45.

brought colour to a tournament or procession), than as the delightful and resourceful artist that he was.

The last artist to be mentioned in this section is Francis Cleyn, a painter from Mecklenburg-Schwerin, who was given the employment of designer to the tapestry manufactory at Mortlake. Cleyn, apart from decorating ceilings in several houses, also designed illustrations for Virgil and Aesop for which, Vertue says, he was paid fifty shillings apiece. The same writer also mentions 'under a neat curious drawing with the pen the portrait (fairly and was neatly writ) Il Famosso Pittore Francesco Clein Miracolo del Secolo and molto stimate dell Re Carolo della Grande Britagna'.

Small, dull, and derivative designs by Cleyn still exist, but more interesting survivals are the pen and bistre drawings by his sons, Francis and John, of the seven Raphael tapestry cartoons, then in the collection of the King. These reduced copies, which are now in the Ashmolean Museum on loan from Wadham College, are dated from 1640 to 1646, and must have been drawn in reverse to take the place of the mirror images previously used by the tapestry weavers at Mortlake.[1] The original cartoons had arrived in England in fragments, and were not joined together until they had served their purpose at the factory, that is during the reign of William III.

It has already been noticed that Cleyn executed drawings for book illustration; and it is perhaps at this point that the small amount of surviving work done in this medium should be examined. The most competent illustrator was Francis Barlow. He produced remarkable illustrations for Aesop's *Fables*—110 plates in all—and there is a further sheet of small drawings in the Ashmolean which suggests that at one time he contemplated doing illustrations for Ovid's *Metamorphoses*. Aesop was particularly suited to Barlow's talent for drawing an entirely real animal-dominated landscape.

The standard of book illustration in England during the seventeenth century was high, if rather over-ornate. The tone is one of elaborate allegory and exaggerated emblematic design, overshadowed by a none too robust classicism. This mixture often results in delightful title-pages, but it is a welcome relief to find a native artist as competent and as free from conventions as Barlow. He removes the uneasy classical attributes from the Englishman, and shows him as a lover of field sports and the country pastimes of the period. Richard Gaywood was another such unaffected artist, who has left a delightful domestic glimpse of a musician, the original drawing for which is in the British Museum (Pl. 33b). It is regrettable that, amongst so many surviving portrait or topographical drawings, there are not more of these intimate

[1] F. J. B. Watson: *On the Early History of Collecting in England*, Burlington Magazine, vol. LXXXV (1944), p. 223 where two of these are reproduced. Evelyn in his *Sculptura* says of these two 'hopeful but now deceased brothers' that in these copies they 'in a fraternal emulation, have done such work as was never yet exceeded by mortal men, either of the former or present age'. I am grateful to Mr Watson and to Dr Margaret Whinney for help over the problem of Cleyn and the Raphael cartoons.

domestic scenes, and that the talent which belonged to the topographical artists did not penetrate the windows of the houses they delineated so accurately. A view or two of the Ouse or the Thames could well have been sacrificed for an observant glance at the inside of a house, a shop, or a tavern. Gaywood's pleasing and rather naïve style can be seen in his engraving of Titian's *Venus and the Organ Player*. This work is dated 1656. That an Englishman should have ventured to engrave such an unpuritanical painting at that date affords, if proof were needed, another refutation of the hard-dying legend that artists stayed sober for the Commonwealth and Protectorate, and then released their pent-up robustness to greet the lowered neckline of the Restoration. A contemporary of Gaywood's was the amateur, Sir Edmund Marmion, whose wash drawings for Francis Quarles' *Argales and Parthenia* are in the Ashmolean. These drawings are feeble, but distinctive enough in style for other examples of this little-known artist's work, should they appear, to be identified.

There was little demand for landscape paintings or drawings from English artists until the nineteenth century, and, although the works of Giorgione, Titian, and Rubens were highly prized by collectors, the landscape in their paintings seems never to have suggested the potential beauties that awaited an artist in the English countryside. Van Dyck alone appears to have appreciated these, and only he has left behind a few exquisite water- and body-colour drawings, which were certainly done during his short and overworked career in England. Examples of these can be found at Chatsworth, in the British Museum (where one is dated 1634), and in the Barber Institute. Rubens seems to have depicted English buildings for the background of his *St George and the Dragon* in Buckingham Palace, but no connected landscape or topographical drawings are known.[1]

The greatest topographical artist of the century was a Bohemian, Wenceslas Hollar. He was born at Prague in 1607, and was perfecting his gifts as an etcher when, in 1636, probably at Cologne, he attracted the notice of the Earl of Arundel, and became attached to his suite. Hollar returned with Arundel to England, and began etching plates after the drawings and paintings in the Earl's collection. Aubrey tells us that Hollar married 'at Arundel House my ladies wayting woman, Mrs Tracy, by whom he had a daughter, that was one of the greatest beauties I have seen; his son by her dyed in the plague, an ingeniose youth; drew delicately.' Hollar also started to etch, soon after his arrival, the first of his views of London and its environs, without which very little would be known of the appearance of the city and its chief buildings at that time, or of the surrounding countryside. Hollar was an indefatigable worker, as is proved by the number of his surviving plates and drawings. The upsets of the Civil War and the death of Arundel affected his fortunes, and from that time until

[1] E. Croft-Murray: *Landscape Background in Rubens's St George. Burlington Magazine*, vol· LXXXIX (1947) p. 89.

his death in 1677 he was never far from penury. It is known that he received only £100 for his year in Tangiers, spent drawing the town and its fortifications for the government.

Hollar is not only a topographer but also the author of the *Ornatus Muliebris* of 1640, which is a most important record of female costume 'from the nobilitie to country women'. This book was later reissued in 1644 as *Aula Veneris*, with a charming frontispiece showing a careful disarray of feminine apparel and articles of toilet. Between 1642 and 1647 he produced the exquisite plates of *Muffs*, perhaps his most charming work, with their wonderful rendering of the texture of fur. Only one drawing of a muff has so far been recorded, and that is in the British Museum (Pl. 33*a*). This small drawing is in its way quite perfect, not only in its loving treatment of texture, but also in the intimate appeal which it can still summon up after three hundred years. Hollar has a secure place in the esteem of all topographers, but it cannot be denied that a few panoramic drawings could well be spared for another muff or glove or costume study. It is in these domestic themes that his greatness is to be recognized.

Drawings by Hollar are mostly in pen and ink, as they were made to be etched, but he also employs at times an attractive water-colour wash. There are also one or two examples to show that he revived silverpoint. The scale of his drawings is very small, but their limitation of size never prevents a largeness of effect.

Hollar's main influence was on the circle of friends at York which centred on the amateur artist, Francis Place. Place regretted that he had not been trained under Hollar, but he was very friendly with him, and followed his methods exactly. It is interesting to see, in Place's letters,[1] the every-day life of this small colony of art-lovers in England at a time when love of art was supposedly at its lowest. The circle included Henry Gyles, the glass painter, who has left a fine *Self Portrait* drawing now in the British Museum, and, among other topographical drawings, an interesting view of *Stonehenge* (Coll. A. P. Oppé). Others were Barlow, William Lodge, John Lambert, and Ralph Thoresby. Place's output was prolific, and his work can be seen in all its strength and limitation in the assemblage at the British Museum, and in the important collection formed by Sir Bruce Ingram.[2] Place was financially independent, and he could work for his own pleasure recording buildings and bridges, especially those of his beloved York. He seems to have enjoyed the sea, and frequently sketched the shipping and coast line. His frequent use of water-colour means that he is best studied in relation to the great artists of this medium, for he is the direct ancestor of Hearne, Girtin, and Turner. Apart from Hollar, the influence of the Dutch topographical school is very noticeable. His most immediately attractive

[1] H. M. Hake, *Walpole Society,* vol. X (1922). The Gyles *Self Portrait* is reproduced *Walpole Society,* vol. XI (1923).

[2] His drawings became more widely known after the Fraser of Hospitalfield, Sale at Sotheby's in 1931.

works are the slight sketches (as opposed to the distant prospects of towns), which include studies of horses and everyday rural scenes. He was a keen fisherman, so it is perhaps suitable that he should be represented here by the hasty sketch of a *Man Fishing* (Pl. 56).

Francis Barlow, to quote Buckeridge's excellent characterization of him, 'was born in Lincolnshire, and at his coming to London, put apprentice to one Shepherd, a face-painter, with whom he lived but few years, because his fancy did not lie that way, his genius leading him wholly to drawing of fowl, fish and other beasts, wherein he arriv'd to that perfection, that had his colouring and penciling been as good as his draught, which was most exact, he might have easily excell'd all that went before him ...'[1]

Barlow has been called the first English sporting artist, and he could also, with equal justice, qualify as the first English landscape artist. The backgrounds to many of his hunting or hawking scenes are reminiscent of the young Gainsborough, and he also anticipates Bewick in his observation of animal life. The birds and beasts of the English countryside had been popular subjects for the borders of mediaeval manuscripts, but Barlow was the first to restore them to their true setting of fields, trees, and ponds. At times his line is inclined to be crude and his animals tend to become too large in proportion to the rest of the composition. It is true that his landscapes owe more than a little to the conventional Dutch backgrounds which appear in contemporary engravings, but, in spite of this, it is obvious that the scenery is English, endowed with a sensivity which could only come from direct observation. There is keenness of observation and a freshness of handling in nearly everything he does. Compared to Barlow, with his intense absorption in the countryside, Place seems a timid urban Sunday-topographer. The medium Barlow employed was never colour, but invariably pen and indian ink wash. This grey wash, when unfaded, gives an almost Chinese effect to many of his drawings. Few of his paintings can be identified now, but one drawing at least (Pl. 27) seems to be adapted from one. Much of his work has suffered from being etched by inferior artists such as Soly and Dudley. The plates done by Francis Place, Hollar, and Barlow himself recapture much more of the spontaneity of the originals. Many of his drawings connect, often in a modified way, with etchings for his book *Severall Wayes of Hunting, Hawking and Fishing*, or for his illustrations to *The Gentleman's Recreation,* and especially for *Various Birds and Beasts,* which were mostly etched by Place. Some of the designs in the latter book must have been admired by Landseer, who certainly took his idea for '*The Cat's Paw*' from one of them.

There are other English topographical draughtsmen, who can be no more than mentioned here: Thomas Johnson, who worked between 1651 and 1675, using mostly pen and wash with slight colour; William Lodge (1649–89), the friend of

[1] B. Buckeridge, Appendix to the *Art of Painting,* by De Piles, 1706.

Francis Place, who sketched in England and Venice, and finally executed a series of natural history drawings; Thomas Manby (*d.* 1695), who drew classical landscapes in the Italian manner; and John Dunstall (active 1644–76), who used water colour on parchment, a type of drawing of which there are two minutely painted examples of great beauty in the British Museum.

No study of English landscape in the seventeenth century would be complete without mentioning Henry Peacham. Peacham was at one time tutor to Arundel's sons, and was considered both a scholar and an artist. Today it is by his two books that he is best remembered, *The Complete Gentleman,* 1643, and *The Gentleman's Exercise,* 1630. A few drawings have been attributed to him, but in nearly all cases it would seem on insufficient grounds, two at least being manifestly Dutch and of the second half of the century. *The Complete Gentleman* was, as Redgrave somewhat tartly remarks, 'much studied by the young gentry of that age, though it does not seem probable that they would gain much art knowledge from it.'[1] Both the books are mines of information on the contemporary attitude to art in general and to 'landskip' in particular, as also on such knowledge as was then accessible of the history of art. Peacham also gives a good survey of the materials then available to an artist, but although he recommends the practice of art in moderation, he cannot bring himself to place it very high among the essential accomplishments of a gentleman. There is almost a note of apology in his defence for its inclusion: 'surely it can bee no disgrace to a great Lord to draw a faire Picture, then to cut his Hawkes meate or play at tennis with his Page'. Nevertheless Peacham did see danger in lack of native encouragement: 'I am sorry that our courtiers and great personages must seek far and near for some Dutchman or Italian to draw their pictures, and invent their demises, our Englishmen being held for vaunients'.

Similarly, John Evelyn in his *Sculptura* 1662, has two revealing remarks to make about the role of drawings:—

'The first and principal manner of DRAWING is that with the PEN; the next with CRAYON, black, white, red, or any of the intermediate colours, upon paper either white or coloured. We will not say much concerning washing with the pencil, or rubbing-in the shades with pastils and dry compositions; because it is not till our disciple be a consummate artist, that he can be edified with designs of this nature, after which they are of excellent use and effect.' And:

'... Since all DRAWING is but as an handmaid and attendant to what you would either GRAVE or PAINT.'

If there was a lack of interest in the landscape painter, there was no such apathy towards the portrait painter, whose services were in continuous demand. To a majority of historians of art the addiction of the English to portraiture has been an

[1] S. Redgrave, *Dictionary of Artists,* London 1878.

embarrassing foible, to be passed over as quickly as possible. This has been true in particular of the seventeenth century, nor is it surprising, in consideration of the preponderance of foreign names and the deterioration of taste that followed the Civil War, that this should have been so. As a result of this portrait consciousness it is only to be expected that the majority of drawings which are known are those made by portrait painters, or later by the fashionable pastellists. Public and private collections are rich in examples of great quality, both in execution and in depth of characterization, but they have hardly been studied at all.

The term 'portrait drawing' embraces so many different types of work that, for clarity, it is best to subdivide into no less than seven categories.[1]

(1) Drawings made for the sitter's retention. There seems to have been some demand for these after the Restoration. Lely, Greenhill, and Mary Beale all made drawings which were finished articles in themselves, and which were sold to their clients.

(2) Studies taken from the life and used towards the completion of the finished painting or engraving; also studies of hands and draperies, which may just have been done from available models in the studio, but are often identifiable with known pictures.

(3) Copies taken for the engraver to work from when he was commissioned to engrave a portrait. These are fairly simple to recognize from their mechanical and dull appearance.

(4) Amateur copies from engravings, and therefore usually in reverse to the original painting. These copies are far more frequently met with than is usually acknowledged, and it is known, both from the journals of Thoresby and Pepys, how popular a family hobby it was to copy the latest prints. Such a good example can be found in Pepys' *Diary* (Nov. 7, 1666) for showing the difference between the engravers' and the amateurs' copies that it is worth quoting it in full: 'Called at Faythorne's to buy some prints for my wife to draw by this winter, where did see my Lady Castlemaine's picture, done by him from Lilly's, in red chalke, and other colours, by which he hath cut it in copper to be printed. The picture in chalk is the finest thing I ever saw in my life I think; and I did desire to buy it; but he says he must keep it awhile to correct his copper plate by, and when that is done he will sell it to me'.

(5) Pastels, which came into fashion at the middle of the century, no doubt through the contact of Faithorne and Samuel Cooper with France, and therefore with the work of Claude Mellan, the Dumoustiers and especially Robert Nanteuil. At first the black and white chalk drawings were only touched with colour, the paper being the middle tint; but later Ashfield and Lutterel enlarged the range of colours,

---

[1] Mr C. F. Bell, *Walpole Society,* vol. V, subdivided seventeenth-century portrait drawings into three classes: his method has been followed here, but enlarged for convenience.

and their work is so highly finished that it is questionable whether they should not be studied as paintings rather than as drawings.

(6) Plumbago drawings on vellum by artists who specialized in minutely worked portrait drawings of small dimension which are best considered in relation to the miniature painters. The practitioners of this medium were David Loggan, who worked mainly in Oxford and London, Robert White, John Faber, and Thomas Forster. These artists frequently signed their work, of which examples are numerous. There are also a great many obvious forgeries, which date back to the earliest years of the twentieth century when there was some demand by collectors for the work of the plumbago artists. The dispersal of a very large collection in 1920, formed by Francis Wellesley, distributed over the market not only numerous very fine examples of seventeenth-century portrait drawing, but also a quantity of extremely suspect ones.

(7) This final category has been almost entirely ignored, and is best described as studies for poses from a studio pattern book. Some such book must have been in use in most artists' studios to enable the sitter to choose fashionable poses in which he or she most fancied themselves, the pattern then being passed to an assistant for the completion of the draperies on the canvas. It is also likely that paintings were recorded in a studio 'Liber Veritatis' to enable duplication without the artists' retention of the completed work. This system would explain the extraordinary number of similar arrangements in existence, distinguishable only by the different heads. A study of these rather mechanical drawings would throw light on the workshop habits of the time. A beginning might be made with the superlative collection of Ramsay drawings at Edinburgh, for amongst them are several drawings, manifestly not by Ramsay, which bear the collector's mark of Joseph van Haecken (or Vanaken), the early eighteenth-century drapery painter. They are mainly copies from Lely, Kneller, and Van Dyck, and would appear to be part of the stock-in-trade of Vanaken. It was, no doubt, part of the studio training to copy the work of the fashionable favourites, and then to draw on these notes when a pose was needed. These copies are often in black chalk on blue paper, and have often very unjustly been called copies after Van Dyck by Lely, if they are from the earlier artist; otherwise they are considered original drawings by Lely, Kneller, or their followers.

After differentiating between the purposes that underlie a portrait drawing, it is necessary to study the development of that medium as a whole and chronologically. Unfortunately, there are few drawings that can be connected with the artists working in England at the same time as, or before, Van Dyck. Van Somer and Mytens have left no drawings of the Court of James I; even more regrettable is the absence of the distinguished hand of Sir Nathaniel Bacon. Drawings have been attributed to Cornelius Johnson, and the attributions may be correct; moreover, according to Vandendoort's inventory of the Royal Collection, Charles I owned a book of drawings by John Hoskins, the miniature painter, whose drawings have never been traced though they may still exist under other names.

Many drawings by Van Dyck, connected with his work in England, are known, and indeed seem to have been prized by English collectors during his lifetime. Sir Peter Lely certainly became possessed of many paintings and drawings from Van Dyck's studio after that artist's death, and his own early Dutch style was modified into an easier elegance by his study of them. A painting such as the one of *Lady Elizabeth Thimbley and Countess Rivers* by Van Dyck, now in the collection of Lord Spencer, is a direct link between the last works of Van Dyck and the middle style of Lely, who, in fact, owned this painting.

How soon after 1635 Van Dyck began taking pupils is not known, but he must have encouraged his pupils to prepare studies in pencil before beginning work on a painting. Undoubtedly his most talented English contemporary was William Dobson (1610–46), who in his short career executed some very gifted and individual work, and, after Hilliard, was the most important native artist who had yet appeared. Dobson, who was the son of a gentleman of St. Albans, had instruction under Peake and Cleyn, and later Van Dyck. He was admired by Charles I and followed the Court to Oxford. His early death was perhaps one of the greatest losses sustained by English art in the seventeenth century. A well illustrated catalogue raisonné of his works is one of the main desiderata of British art history. Up to the present no drawing can be given to Dobson with absolute certainty; that in the collection of Mr. Brinsley Ford (Pl. 18), is close to Dobson, but the general feeling of this work is perhaps nearer to the swagger of Isaac Fuller (1606–72). The full-length man (Pl. 19) is almost certainly a contemporary copy of an extant painting by Van Dyck. Neither Dobson nor Fuller can have underrated the importance of drawings, both to an artist's work and for the collector: they both painted portraits of sitters holding drawings. Dobson has shown the large man called Sir Balthasar Gerbier (himself a talented draughtsman, as can be seen in his miniature drawing of the young *Charles I* at South Kensington) in the remarkable triple group in the Northumberland Collection, holding a very mannerist drawing of a female figure. Fuller, in his over life-size *Self Portrait when Drunk,* at Oxford, has depicted himself holding a drawing of two nude children. Very little of Fuller's painting has survived, and his murals in London and Oxford have perished. His portraits, though coarsely painted, have a bold and brassy quality about them, and a delicacy of facial modelling which is as sensitive as it is unexpected. The head for this *Self Portrait* (Pl. 21) in the Victoria and Albert Museum seems, on the evidence of style, to be the original study, not merely a later copy made for engraving, for the curious cross hatching in it is the same as in the two drawings attributed to him in the British Museum. Sir Robert Witt owns a *Male Nude Study,* which is signed and dated presumably by Fuller's son, but so little is known of the latter that no more can be done than to record its existence. It is greatly to be regretted that there are not more drawings by Dobson and Fuller, both of whom are vital links in the continuity of British portrait painting into the eighteenth century. It is possible that a careful sifting of Van Dyck's drawings may yet yield some hitherto wrongly named, which are yet of sufficient distinction to be given to Dobson.

Robert Walker (c. 1619–58) is another native artist of merit, who can only be credited with a single drawing, and that so bad that it seems almost harsh to persist in doing so. This head of the *1st Duchess of Beaufort* has every appearance of being the original study for her portrait at Badminton, and not merely a copy made about the same time by a lesser hand. So many drawings have been wrongly attributed to Walker that this head, which has serious claim to be considered autograph, must be published (Pl. 20) in spite of its obvious defects.

William Faithorne (1616–91)[1] is chiefly famous as the most skilful English engraver of his time, but he also worked as a pastellist, doing highly finished portraits. Plates 24 and 25 are good examples of his heavy and yet sensitive style. His finest drawing, the plumbago and wash drawing of his friend, *John Aubrey* (Pl. 22), is in the Ashmolean.

Perhaps the most beautiful individual portrait drawing of the century executed in England is by the miniature painter, Samuel Cooper (1609–72), and is also at Oxford (Pl. 23). No other example of this quality is known elsewhere: the original of the *Self Portrait* in the Victoria and Albert is lost, and two heads of *Charles II* at Windsor, though good, are not of the same sensitivity.[2] The Oxford drawing is consistent with the line and style that one would expect from the artist of the two unfinished miniatures at Windsor of *Lady Castlemaine* and the *Duke of Monmouth*.

Just as Van Dyck has reproduced for all time the aloof and aristocratic background of the reign of Charles I, so Sir Peter Lely (1618–80) has fixed in our minds the visual image of the relaxed and raffish Court which followed the Restoration.

The Court which Lely served had little or no pretensions to elegance, but in fact it adopted at Whitehall an unhappy imitation of the Classical Arcadia of Versailles. Those fashionable conventions, which seem vulgar and ridiculous after three hundred years, taxed the skill of all contemporary artists. Lely, and later Kneller, had to contend with the wig, which extinguished a man's face, and made everyone take on a monotonous family likeness; while all the women demanded décolleté dresses,

[1] Biographical details and information about Faithorne's work are readily accessible in books on English engraving, or in Mr A. M. Hind's article in the *Connoisseur,* vol. XCII (1933), p. 92.

[2] Reproduced by Cundall, *Connoisseur,* vol. XCII, 1933, pages 75 and 127. The medium of these two drawings, black chalk on dark paper, makes satisfactory reproduction difficult. These drawings were executed for the Inauguration medal of 1660. In this connection it is worth noting that the medallist, Thomas Simon, was a competent draughtsman, as can be seen from the reproductions in *Walpole Society,* vol. XXVIII where his sketch book was published by Mr Derek Allen.

sheep and an urn as essential to the finished painting. These two painters responded to fashion as they found it, became prosperous, and killed their own reputations by the replicas and accessory painting, done by other and second-rate painters, in their workshops.

A new assessment of Lely's work is very necessary. At his best he shows admirable modelling and characterization, especially with men, and above all a varied and delicate colour sense. Given sitters who interested him, he could produce remarkable portraits. Both Pope, in his famous lines, and Lady Mary Wortley Montagu, with her equally well-known

'Your nightgown fastened with a single pin
Fancy improved the wondrous charms within',

seized on the superficial approach to Lely. In his drawings it is possible to see him freed from all the insincere trappings of fashion.

As a draughtsman Lely has been admired, but quickly passed over, although his work in this medium is not rare. On further examination it becomes plain that he must take a high place, in a European setting, amongst the seventeenth-century portrait draughtsmen. Nevertheless, a painter writing recently could still say that Lely 'produced a monotonous series of third-rate portrait drawings, which became steadily worse'.[1]

Lely's career is not at all clear, and presents many problems. Briefly, he came to England sometime between 1641 and 1643. In 1647 he painted the moving portrait of *Charles I and the Duke of York* at Syon, and there are no certain dateable paintings before this. In the same house is still to be found his faithful copy of Van Dyck's *Algernon Percy,* which shows just how well he understood that artist's style and technique; and certainly during the Civil War Lely perfected his style from the older artist's work. It is not true to say his style was stiff and sedate, as befitted a painter during the Commonwealth, and was later altered for the changed times. In fact, he appears to have painted during the 50's surprisingly unpuritanical portraits, as well as his subject pieces. In 1656 Lely had permission to visit Holland, and the next four years of his life are mysterious, though it seems almost certain that he returned within two years. He became rich early in his career and lived in great state, and indeed, though it is not clear from the confusing entries, he seems to have dabbled in moneylending, and had Charles II as a very substantial debtor by 1661.

After Lely's death in 1682 his executor, Roger North, had the task of selling his enormous and justly famous collection of drawings, which had been enriched by the disposal of Van Dyck's studio and the collections of Arundel and Charles I.

---

[1] M. Ayrton: *British Drawings,* London 1946. As their chronology is not at all clear it could equally well be said that Lely's drawings begin badly and get better. In fact they nearly all keep to a respectable standard.

There is more than a hint given by Constantin Huygens, in his account of his interview with Queen Mary and his sight of the Royal drawings, that Lely enriched his own collection by fraud. 'Afterwards saw other books of Italian drawings in which it looked very much as if something had been stolen from them, and it was stated that Lilly, having borrowed the books from Chiffins, had gone thoroughly to work and taken originals out of them, putting in copies made by his people.'[1] This sounds most unlikely, but shows that Lely's passion for collecting drawings had not been forgotten in the Stuart family. He was the first, with Lanier and Lankrink, of those famous English painter-collectors who include Richardson, Hudson, Reynolds, West and Lawrence.

Roger North has left an account of his own method of marking all the drawings sold. 'I got a stamp, P. L., and with a little printing ink, I stamped every individual paper.' This accounts for the mark appearing on drawings by Lely, which were still in the studio at the time of his death, as well as on those he collected.[2]

Few of Lely's drawings can be dated with accuracy. Evidence of costume and pose, however, would seem to indicate that they begin soon after he came to London, and were to continue until his death. Vertue writes of his 'fine freedom of pencill, especially at the last'. The medium he employed was black or coloured chalks on buff or blue paper, heightened with white, which gave him great breadth of handling. Sometimes he obtains his effect by a few broad strokes followed by a careful working up with slight colour; at other times it is most remarkable to see with how few lines and what minimum of working he achieves it.

Chalk portraits form the bulk of his work. They are easily distinguishable from the less skilled and heavier work of his English and Dutch contemporaries. None the less, Lely has been credited with a great many dull and worthless works, as well as those which have been so rubbed and reworked as to be virtually spurious. His portrait drawings are never connected with paintings, and were therefore made not as working studies, as in the case of Holbein, but for pleasure, and more often for the sitter's retention and purchase. The highly finished state of many of them confirms this view, and in the sale catalogue of 'Original Drawings and Pictures of Sir Peter Lely's own hand' can be found the following entry, 'Craions of Sir Peter Lely in ebony frames:'

'Several heads of Lady Carnarvon.
One of the Lord Askot.
One of the late Lady Chesterfield.

[1] From transcript of *Journal of C. Huygens.* Published 1876, p. 326.
[2] *Executors Account Book of Sir Peter Lely 1679–1691.* British Museum Ad. 16174. An album of drawings by Lely figures in Jonathan Richardson's sale. Whether it was a sketch book or merely made up of his drawings is not clear. Lely drawings with Richardson's mark are very rarely found.

INTRODUCTION

The Countess of Southaske.
The Lady Diana Thynne.
Several of Mrs Franklyn.
Mrs Gratiana.
Sir Philip Parker.
Mr Tho. Killigrew.
Mr Gibson.
A Craion Head of an Italian.'[1]

None of the above listed works can be recognized today, for they have lost their identity as thoroughly, probably, as the ladies in the British Museum or Windsor Series. The name of Barbara Villiers, Lady Castlemaine (later Duchess of Cleveland) figures in catalogue entries, frequently but erroneously. The features of this most rapacious of the mistresses of Charles II are well-known, and can be found in some of the finest paintings by Lely, Samuel Cooper, and J. M. Wright: in fact an iconography of this termagant woman would supply an excellent guide to the best of Restoration painting, but not one drawing of her by Lely can be traced. The nearest is that in the collection of Mr L. G. Duke, which depicts her and her infant as the *Virgin and Child,* but this does not seem to be of sufficient quality to be by Lely himself. Certain of his sitters can be identified, including his own early *Self Portrait* (Pl. 38), still in the possession of his descendants, together with a much rubbed portrait of his wife, Ursula, and one of their son. Sir Neil Malcolm owns an earlier *Self Portrait,* while in the British Museum are portraits of *Lauderdale, Greenhill,* and *Waller.*[2]

Of actual studies for paintings there are few. The double portrait drawing at Munich which connects with two existing single portraits seems to be only an example of a pose pattern. The Ashmolean, Fitzwilliam, and Sir Robert Witt own studies of hands and drapery for known compositions. Charles Beale records in his journal: 'Mr Lely dead colour'd my son Charles picture—took a drawing upon paper after an Indian gown which he had put on his back, in order to the finishing the drapery of it. Aug. 1674.' There is also a drawing for the full length portrait of the Duke of Norfolk.

Lely executed, probably during the late 1650's, several historic paintings, a few of which have been recognized. Only one non-portrait drawing has come to light (Pl. 46), a study for his *Susanna and the Elders.* At various times one or two others have been attributed to him, but there seems very little internal or external evidence for accepting them.[3] One further drawing deserves consideration in this context, the

---

[1] *Sir Peter Lely's Collection, Burlington Magazine,* vol. LXXXIII (1943).

[2] There are in existence not very deceptive copies of both the *Waller* and the *Lauderdale* in which the monogram has also been copied.

[3] The frontispiece to Lovelace's *Lucasta,* 1649 is inscribed 'P. Lilly Inv. W. Faithorne sculp. Paris.' The lady represented is identified on a proof in the British Museum as 'Lucy Sacheverall'. This is a very charming Lely design, and is one more piece of evidence that Plate 47 is not by him.

Lady at a Fountain in the Ashmolean (Pl. 47). Although at first sight this composition appears to have several characteristics of Lely, it must be by an entirely different hand. It is not impossible that it may be by Lely's rival collector of drawings, Prosper Henry Lankrink (1628–92), on the somewhat flimsy evidence of the mezzotint after his *Nymphs Bathing*.[1] It is always a dangerous habit to find names for drawings too readily, and, with the little that is known of Lankrink's work, this drawing could be placed, with an equal amount of uncertainty, on almost any shadowy doorstep, even one as remote as that of the fair amateur celebrated by Dryden, Mistress Anne Killigrew.

Lely's greatest achievement as a draughtsman are the drawings of the Garter Knights and Officials, which were at one time believed to be by Van Dyck. In style and costume they point conclusively to Lely, and are now universally accepted as his work (Pl. 34–37).

The purpose this series was to serve is now obscure: there is no connection with the 1671 Hollar engraving of the Garter Procession, or any other illustration. They may have been a guide to the dress worn by the various officers of the order, which the artist was asked to produce at the revival of the ceremony after the Restoration. During the years of the Civil War and Commonwealth memory of these things had probably grown dim, and the renewal of the costume, at the hands of Lely, using whatever evidence he could call on, was probably the best solution for both robe-makers and participants. It is quite possible that some of the clothes may even have been designed by Lely.

The other possibility, much more unlikely, is that they were the working drawings for a scheme of decoration. Van Dyck had proposed a similar idea for Whitehall, and had gone so far as to make a large grisaille sketch of a *Procession of the Knights of the Garter*. The Civil War and Van Dyck's death prevented this idea from maturing, but it was Lely who bought the sketch at the Royal sale. As it figures later in his own sale, it must be assumed that it was not surrendered to the King, with his other purchases, at the Restoration. It now belongs to the Duke of Rutland.[2] The scene is lightly and delicately worked, but there is no connection between this and the Lely drawings. Perhaps, then, Lely had a scheme for a full-scale mural work, as he had once before during the Commonwealth, and for that reason was allowed to retain the Van Dyck. The decoration of St. George's Hall at Windsor may have been intended for the setting, for nothing could be more suitable, along the walls, than a procession of the Knights. If there is any truth in this theory, the scheme came to nothing, and it was Verrio who eventually covered Windsor with his fluent

---

[1] *P. H. Lankrink's Collection, Burlington Magazine*, vol. LXXXVI (1945), p. 29 where the mezzotint is reproduced together with the only painting that can at the moment be ascribed to him.

[2] This painting has never been reproduced.

allegories. Whatever the purpose for which these drawings were made, they remain a perpetual monument to Lely's talent.

The fashion for pastels having once been set by Lely and Faithorne, there was no lack of followers. It is not hard to find scores of examples, though no one appears to have attained the delicacy of Lely. Some carried the minute finishing to such an extent that the lines of the draughtsman disappear under the weight of chalk. These highly finished pastels, as they appear on the market, are usually distributed equally but indiscriminately between Ashfield and Lutterel.

There are no recognizable drawings by Lely's most gifted contemporaries, J. M. Wright, Gerard Soest, Jacob Huysmans, John Riley and William Wissing. This is particularly unfortunate in the case of Riley (1649–91), who was a pupil of Fuller and Soest, the link between these latter artists, through Hudson and Richardson, with Reynolds. One drawing in the British Museum has an inscription assigning it to an almost forgotten brother mentioned by Vertue. The *Nude Man,* in the collection of Mr. A. P. Oppé, which has a traditional ascription to Riley, can never be properly assessed until further examples come to light. There are, however, a series of female heads, chalk on dark paper, which are usually catalogued as by Riley. Of these the two most beautiful are in the Victoria and Albert Museum and the collection of Sir Bruce Ingram. There can be little doubt that, on the grounds of hair-style and costume, they must be by an artist working mainly in the first years of the eighteenth century, probably Michael Dahl, who came to England in 1678 and lived on until 1743. Others, obviously by the same hand, are in fact given to Dahl in the British Museum, and, though perhaps more sensitive than might be expected from his paintings, are consistent with his style.

The work of Lely's pupils is more easily recognized. There is a signed and rather lifeless pastel by Henry Tilson in the British Museum. It is known that Tilson was the artist called in when Dr Busby, the great Headmaster of Westminster School, died, to draw his head for posthumous portraits and busts. It is likely that Dahl's large portrait of Busby, still at the school, was executed from one of these drawings. Vertue notes of Tilson that he was 'much more acceptable to the curious in art, than he was to a Mistress whom he had courted for a long time till at length, through a Melancholy Habit of body contracted by her unkindness, and a sedentary life he shot himself with a pistol to the Heart. He had a particular genius for crayons, in which he performed admirably well, after the pictures of Correggio, Titian and the Caracci, while he was in Rome'.[1]

The most interesting follower of Lely was John Greenhill (? 1644–76), an

---

[1] Some of the family paintings, mentioned by Vertue, are still in the possession of Tilson's descendants, but it has not been possible to trace any other drawings, beyond one of *Francesco Guiseppe Borri,* done in Rome in 1687 which is in the Hansteen Collection in Oslo. I am grateful to Mr Waterhouse for drawing my attention to this drawing.

Englishman, whose father was Clerk to the Chapter at Salisbury. He was an in-
dustrious pupil of Lely, and then fell into bad company and was debauched, and
died when aged only about thirty-two. There are several references to his proficiency
as a draughtsman. Vertue records 'from the life—Heads done in crayons by Greenhill, says Mr (Tho.) Gibson that he had seen with great skill and perfection equal to
any master whatever.' And again 'Mr Blow a relation had his own portrait in
a wigg. Mrs G. by Lely and many drawings and other pictures by Greenhill'.
Today there are only five drawings certainly his:[1] His *Self Portrait* in the British
Museum (Pl. 49), signed with a monogram, which is interesting to compare with
Lely's portrait of him (Pl. 48); the Oxford *Portrait of a Lady*, and the drawing of
William Smith at Port Eliot; and the portraits of *Joseph Harris as Wolsey* at Magdalen,
and *Betterton as Bajazet* at Kingston Lacy. All these conform closely with his own
etching of his brother in the Ashmolean,[2] and make a solid core for testing other
drawings which might be given to him. William Cartwright, who left his collection
to Dulwich in 1688, recorded in his MS. Catalogue the prices he paid to Greenhill
for three crayons, £2 for one and £3 for each of the others, and states that they were
'covered with glass'.[3]

The Gibsons, whose exact family relationship one to another is hard to disentangle, and Mary Beale and her son complete the main set of Lely's followers and
pupils. Richard Gibson (1615–90) was a dwarf, who became a miniature painter
and drawing instructor to the future Queens, Mary and Anne. He married a lady
the same height as himself, 3 ft. 10 in., and begot nine normal-sized children. Waller
wrote a charming poem to celebrate this marriage of true bodies:

'Design or chance makes others wive,
but nature did this match contrive;
Eve might as well have Adam fled,
As she deny'd her little bed
To him, for whom Heav'n seem'd to frame,
And measure out his only Dame—'

One pastel is certainly by Gibson, the *Young Girl* in the British Museum.[4] It has
usually been assumed that his kinsman, William Gibson, was the only Gibson to
collect drawings and that it was he who was the main purchaser at Lely's sale. There
is, however, evidence on the reverse of a drawing at Oxford, by Polidoro Caldara

[1] The drawings at Peckforton, mentioned by Cust, have vanished, and the *Earl of Bristol* at South Kensington
is to be discounted on the grounds of its dissimilarity to those that are certainly autograph.
[2] British Museum Counter Proof, reproduced *Connoisseur,* vol. XCII (1933) p. 105.
[3] No longer to be found at Dulwich. *Catalogue of the Pictures at Dulwich* 1926, p. 204.
[4] Reproduced in J. J. Foster, *Samuel Cooper,* Pl. LXIII.

(retouched by Rubens) that Richard Gibson was also a collector. This evidence is in the handwriting of Jonathan Richardson the Younger.[1] It may be necessary to readjust the collecting activities of the two Gibsons. The elder Richardson and probably the 2nd Duke of Devonshire may have bought from the widow of the dwarf some time before her death in 1709; later, in 1733, both Richardson and the 3rd Duke of Devonshire certainly purchased from another widow, probably the relict of William Gibson.[2] A third Gibson was Edward, who is responsible for the flamboyant *Self Portrait* (Pl. 58), which comes as a welcome relief to the well known, unvaried patterns of the century. He 'first painted portraits in oil but afterwards finding more encouragement in craions, his genius lying that way, he made a considerable progress.'[3]

Mary Beale, whose maiden name was Craddock, came from Suffolk, and married Charles Beale, an artist and colourman. Several of the notebooks kept by her husband, whose whole life seems to have revolved round his wife's career, are extant, and from these a great deal is known about her activities. She copied works by Van Dyck and Lely for her instruction, and had the hierarchy of the Church as her main patrons. There is also a series of letters in the Bodleian, sent by Flatman to Charles Beale, which make it plain that he considered Mrs Beale his pupil, and that he bought his colours from Beale.[4] To complete this extensive documentation (so lacking for other artists), her sketch-book at South Kensington contains copies after both Van Dyck and Lely, as well as her own drawings, and a few, mainly from casts, by her son, Charles. She also seems to have been prolific in the production of red chalk portraits, several score of which are scattered over public and private collections. These are not only of her distinguished clients, but also of humbler citizens, especially leather workers. This plethora of work and documentation has given her too great a fame, and her red chalk drawings have come almost to typify the style of the English seventeenth-century draughtsmen. Her work for the most part lacks animation and sensitivity, and possesses only a boring competency.

Her son Charles, who was also a painter, produced very similar drawings (several of which are signed with his monogram), so similar in fact, that it is almost impossible to distinguish them from his mother's.

The mysterious T. Thrumpton, who is responsible for the signed Oxford double-sided drawing (Pl. 52), should be mentioned. His work is of sufficient

---

[1] The inscription runs: 'This drawing was bought of the widow of Gibson the miniature painter, commonly known by the name of the Dwarf who esteemed it the capital Drawing of his whole Collection as the widow Gibson told Mr Richardson, who himself used to account it superior to the rest of his Pollidores, Touched by Rubens, of which however he had several mainly out of the Arundell Collection, from whence also this is supposed to have come as Gibson is known to have procured many of them'. According to the *Dictionary of National Biography* the widow of the Dwarf died in 1709 aged 89.

[2] F. J. B. Watson, *On the early History of Collecting in England, Burlington Magazine*, vol. LXXXV (1944) p. 224, who shows that both Richardsons purchased drawings from another Gibson widow in 1733.

[3] Buckeridge: *op. cit.*, p. 378.   [4] Rawlinson Letter, CIV.

quality and individuality to make it recognizable. There is also in the collection of Lady Sybil Grant a most sensitive pastel of John Locke, signed by Sylvester Brownover, an artist no less elusive than Thrumpton, but who is known to have been a servant of Locke's.

Although it may be stated that Lely and his followers worked in coloured chalk, Edward Lutterel and Edmund Ashfield can be claimed almost wholly as pastellists. They enlarged the range of colours available, and applied them thickly, so that their portraits take on many of the characteristics of oil paintings. Lutterel went even further with pastels on copper surfaces, such as the *Duke of Bedford* in the National Portrait Gallery, or the *Unknown Man* in Dublin. He usually scratched on his signature with a stylus. His work on paper is lighter in tone than that of his instructor, Ashfield, and looser and more smudged in technique. Very often, too, some fault in the paper or its preparation causes it to look patchy and creased. Examples of this are the *Charles II* (Pl. 59), in the collection of Mr Duke, and the *James II* in the collection of Sir Bruce Ingram. Ashfield, though much heavier, has a greater ability in rendering the texture of hair and clothing. He is supposed to have been a pupil of J. M. Wright, and was rated so highly by his contemporaries that he could command £10 for his portraits. Perfect examples of his finished technique are preserved in the collection of Mr W. Plowden (Pl. 60), and at Ham House. Although it has become a habit loosely to attribute all these heavier pastels to Ashfield and Lutterel, their two styles are readily distinguishable. Another hand certainly is frequently found which uses a harsh shade of pink for flesh and drapery. These pastels are given in a haphazard way to Lely, whose innate taste and colour sense would have eschewed the pink, or to Cooper and Lutterel. Whoever this artist may have been he has had a disastrous posthumous effect on the work of his contemporaries, for several ardent retouchers have been smitten with the same delight in this pink, and have brought back garish carnations to many a genuine, if faded, Lely or Ashfield.

The plumbago artists already referred to fall outside the scope of this introduction; but it is worth quoting a remark by John Aubrey in his *Brief Lives:* 'This last month I persuaded him (Sir William Petty) to sitt to Mr Loggan, the graver, whom I forthwith went for myselfe, and he drewe it just before goeing into Ireland & 'tis very like him. But about 1659, he had a picture in miniature drawne by his friend and mine, Mr Samuel Cowper (Prince of limners of his age), one of the likest that ever he drew'. A plumbago portrait appears to have been regarded as a pleasant and cheaper memento of a person, but in no way did it usurp the popularity of the miniature or pastel.

The pastel and the plumbago were the new fashion of the century, but whereas the pastel was to find favour for many years and to gain impetus from the remarkable work of La Tour and Liotard, the plumbago slipped out of fashion as suddenly and as quietly as it had come in—a pleasing, if monotonous, interlude amidst the bravura of chalk portraits.

The last years of the Stuart dynasty were dominated in portraiture by Godfrey Kneller (1646/49–1723), a native of Lübeck, who came to London in 1675, and quickly made a reputation that was to last well into the eighteenth century. On Lely's death he had no rival, and became the chief painter to the Court. Kneller is, in himself and his atelier, almost the last example of the mediaeval workshop system. Under him portrait painting became a finished and efficient piece of commercial mass production. Naturally his reputation has suffered under the huge weight of wigs and négligés that this over-productiveness has imposed on the critical faculty of time. Walpole hit some of the truth when he said 'where he offered one picture to fame he sacrificed twenty to lucre'. Kneller, at his best, in such portraits as his *Matthew Prior* at Trinity, Cambridge, or his *3rd Earl of Leicester* at Penshurst, is a painter of subtlety and depth. His heads show often the greatest care in modelling, and are painted with rich, free, liquid brush strokes; but he lacks the taste and colour sense of Lely, and is a far less able draughtsman. His portrait drawings appear always to be connected in some way with the production of a painting, and were not finished studies in themselves like those of Lely. Although there are two manuscript accounts in existence of Lely's methods of painting, there is no mention of the use of drawings in either of them. In Kneller's case, however, an illuminating letter exists from Pope to Lady Mary Wortley Montagu in answer to her request that he should arrange a sitting with Kneller for her: 'Upon conferring with Kneller I find he thinks it absolutely necessary to draw the face first, which he says can never be set right on the figure if the drapery and posture be finished before. To give you as little trouble as possible he proposes to draw your face with crayons and finish it up at your own house in a morning; from whence he will transfer it to the canvas, so that you need not go to sit at his house. This, it must be observed, is a manner in which they seldom draw any but crowned heads; and I observe it with secret pride and pleasure. Be so kind as to tell me if he should do this tomorrow at twelve.'[1]

Unfortunately a great many amateur and engravers' drawings have become absorbed into Kneller's work, and it is not at all easy to recognize his portrait style which, in any case, is extremely variable.[2] The *Head of a Young Man*, belonging to Sir Robert Witt (Pl. 63), is so good that there is almost a suspicion that it might be by the young Ramsay, while, on the other hand, the drawing of *Louis XIV* at

---

[1] W. T. Whitley, *Artists and their Friends in England,* London, 1928, vol. I, p. 5.

[2] As an example, the drawing called the *1st Duke of Marlborough* at South Kensington is, in fact, a drawing in reverse of the Kit Cat portrait of the *6th Duke of Somerset.*

Windsor, for the painting now at Drayton and fully inscribed as the actual study made by Kneller at Versailles, is so wooden as to seem incompatible with some of his signed drawings.

Apart from his portrait drawings there are a few copies after the Old Masters, such as the *Man in Armour* in the British Museum, or the *Head of St. Jerome* at Edinburgh.[1] It would be interesting if any Kneller copies of Rembrandt and Bol were to come to light, as he is reliably stated to have been their pupil in Amsterdam. Kneller worked out his own formula for his portraits, which owed more than a little to the Titian-Van Dyck tradition, and to his contact with Bernini and Maratta in Rome, and was continued, in the hands of his more mediocre followers, until the time of other portrait painters Reynolds and Gainsborough.

John Vanderbank is worth studying in detail, for he could draw, apart from his better known and rather scratchy ink figure studies, a hand as attractive and sensitive as Plate 63. Vertue ranked him 'in the art of drawing and painting, of all men born in this nation superior in skill.' Vanderbank, like all promising native artists, such as Dobson, Walker, Greenhill and Riley, died in early middle age. The reproving finger of Redgrave, in his *Dictionary of Artists,* is only too apparent as he unfolds his tales of debauchery and death that cut short many an artist's career before he had shown his full power. This high rate of mortality can in no way be used as an excuse for the non-emergence of an English School, but it cannot be overlooked that, whenever an English artist appeared who seemed to have the largeness of understanding and the mastery of his medium to make him more than equal to his foreign contemporaries, he left the scene early, leaving behind a small number of fine works and a host of speculations as to what his future and influence might have meant to British Art.

The century culminates in fact with the work of the great collector of drawings, Jonathan Richardson (1665–1745), and of Sir James Thornhill (1675–1734). Not only does Richardson conclude the plumbago tradition, but his large chalk portrait drawings are entirely seventeenth century in feeling, though none can be traced before 1700. His work tends to be monotonous, but there is a sense of style and swagger, especially in his many self portraits, which is attractive.

The other Englishman, James Thornhill (1675–1734), richly deserves a book to himself, for he has left behind many vigorous and lively sketches for decorative schemes. In Thornhill and his contemporaries the first signs of the real emancipation of the English School are apparent. This can be seen in the activities of clubs of artists and in the setting up of the first Academy with a life school, of which Kneller was the first Governor and Thornhill the second. Travel led to a more enlightened patronage and more enlightened painters, so that as the old fashions

[1] Taken from the painting by Guercino of *St Jerome,* now in the collection of Mr Denis Mahon.

of the seventeenth century were thrown off, the new ones of the eighteenth century grew in favour and began to take lasting shape. It is possible to look back beyond the eighteenth and nineteenth century portrait- and landscape-painters to the struggles and frustrations of the sixteenth and seventeenth centuries, and to admire, in the face of fashion and prejudice, much that was accomplished by the native artists and by those from abroad who worked mainly in England,—not least their drawings.

CATALOGUE OF PLATES

Measurements are given in centimetres, followed by inches

1. UNKNOWN FOLLOWER OF HANS HOLBEIN.

KING HENRY VIII (1491–1547). Munich, Graphische Sammlung.

Black and coloured chalk on white paper tinted with red; 31 × 25 (12¼ × 9¾).

Lit. Ganz: *Die Handzeichnungen Hans Holbein d. J.*, 1937, p. 79 (CI).

This drawing is a copy from the wall painting by Holbein at Whitehall Palace, which was destroyed in the fire of 1689. This contained four whole-length figures, Henry VIII, his wife, Jane Seymour, and his father and mother, Henry VII and Elizabeth of York. The original cartoon for part of this work is preserved at Chatsworth, and shows the King nearly in profile. The finished full-face painting became the prototype for many representations by other artists in the sixteenth and seventeenth centuries. While the painting, which was in the privy chamber, was in existence it made a great impression, even in its later and more dilapidated days, on all who saw it, and no doubt kept Holbein's name fresher in people's minds than that of most artists. It may also in some way account for the preservation both of the Holbein drawings at Windsor and the Chatsworth cartoon. It is not without interest to note, in connection with the vexed question of how the drawings returned to the Royal Collection after Arundel's death, that it was Charles II who ordered the small copy by Leemput, which is now preserved at Hampton Court, of the Whitehall painting. If Charles II valued the great Holbein so much, he may well have been persuaded by Lely to buy the drawings, as is often assumed.

2. UNKNOWN ENGLISH ARTIST.

HENRY HOWARD, EARL OF SURREY (1517–1547). H.M. The King

Metal point and chalk on pink priming; 19 × 14 (7½ × 5½). Inscribed (wrongly) *Tho Howard..* *E. of Surrey.*

Lit. Parker: *The Drawings of Hans Holbein in the Collection of H.M. the King at Windsor Castle*, Phaidon, 1945 (Cat. No. 83 repr.). For drawings of Surrey by Holbein see the same volume (Cat. Nos. 17 and 29).

3. UNKNOWN ENGLISH ARTIST.

HENRY HOWARD, EARL OF SURREY (1517–1547). New York, Morgan Library.

Metal point and chalk on pink priming; 14 × 10 (5½ × 3¾).

Collections: (?) Arundel, Thane, Fairfax Murray (259 of Publication of Fairfax Murray drawings).

In the inscription, 'Hen' is an emendation for 'Tho'., which can be discerned underneath. This is the drawing of the Earl of Surrey in profile, 'No. 100', which, from the diagram in Vertue's Catalogue of 1743, published by Bathoe, 1758, is known to have hung in Queen Caroline's 'Holbein Closet'. How this drawing left the Royal Collection is not clear. Chamberlaine may have removed it as a spurious item. See note to Plate 4.

Lit. Parker: *Holbein,* page 18 and note[7].

4. UNKNOWN ENGLISH ARTIST.

BISHOP JOHN FISHER (1459–1535). National Portrait Gallery.

Oils on transparent paper, silhouetted; 20·5 × 19 (8 × 7½).

Collections: John Chamberlaine, Rev. Thomas Bancroft, John Wolstenholme. Sold Sotheby's, 1. iv. 36 (lot 6).

There is a letter in existence, from Wolstenholme, written when the drawing was offered to the Portrait Gallery (which refused it) in 1892. In this he says that this portrait with many others came into the possession of his grandfather (The Rev. Thomas Bancroft, M.A., Head Master of the King's School, Chester) in 1795–7 from a 'noted collector and archaeologist, Mr Chamberlaine, Most of the paintings were discovered in an old cabinet discarded from Kensington Palace and bought by Chamberlaine. Mr Bancroft and he were close personal friends and in this manner he became the owner. I wish to show that they have been in the continuous possession of our family since 1797 and not collected here and there'. This collection, before it was dispersed, included besides the Fisher, one called *Bishop Bonner* (now in Private Collection); a lady, wrongly called *Mary I* (Coll. Sir Bruce Ingram); *George Talbot, Earl of Shrewsbury* (National Portrait Gallery); an *Ecclesiastic* (National Portrait Gallery); and one called *Charles IX* (whereabouts unknown). These are all oils on paper. The crayon portraits included *Queen Elizabeth in a yellow Wig* (National Portrait Gallery), a *Profile of Edward VI* (whereabouts unknown), and *Archbishop Warham* (Coll. Messrs. Agnew). This last is certainly not by Holbein himself.

It is improbable that two sets of Holbeinesque drawings should have been discovered in a piece of furniture at Kensington. Perhaps Chamberlaine, who gave the drawings to Bancroft, told his friend of Queen Caroline's discovery of the Windsor drawings, and the family, over a period, grafted the story on to their own collection. It would be interesting to know how Chamberlaine obtained them. It is possible he removed them, when he became Royal Librarian in 1791, from the other Holbein drawings on the grounds that they were not autograph. If this was the case, they would have had the same history as the Windsor drawings, and been discovered by Queen Caroline. Vertue mentions them (*Walpole Society* vol. IV, p. 65) 'in a large book of prints pasted in—an old drawing of G. Talbot Earl of Shrewsbury only the face. ob. 1590. The face only of Bp. Fisher after Holbein . . . a Judge Exchequer 1582 his collar on. face of Queen Mary I'. It is not known where he saw them.

Finally, it should be remarked that this tracing of Fisher is closer in features to the drawing in the British Museum, attributed to Holbein, than to the better known, and certainly autograph one, at Windsor. Wolstenholme declared, in another letter, that his Fisher had been in the sale of Richardson's Collection, which is impossible if its provenance is the same as those at Windsor. There is no trace of its having been his; Richardson did, however, own the British Museum *Fisher*. This again may be another family error, and suggests that someone had already connected the drawing and the tracing.

5. NICHOLAS HILLIARD, B. 1547 D. 1619.
DESIGN FOR THE OBVERSE OF QUEEN ELIZABETH'S GREAT SEAL OF IRELAND.   British Museum.

Inscribed *Elisabet D. G. Anglie Fra et Hibernie Regina*.

Pen and ink and wash over pencil; circular diam. 12·8 (5¼).

Collection: P. Gellatly.

Lit. Reynolds: *Hilliard and Oliver*, Victoria and Albert Museum Handbooks, 1947, p. 36, where a bibliography is given.

6. NICHOLAS HILLIARD.
AN ELIZABETHAN LADY IN COURT COSTUME.   Victoria and Albert Museum.

? Signed in lower right-hand corner (a tear and collector's mark obscure this).

Pen and ink and pencil; 13 × 11 (5 × 4¼).
Collections: Francis Wellesley; A. G. B. Russell.

7. ISAAC OLIVER, B. *c.* 1556. D. 1617.
    QUEEN ELIZABETH (1553–1603).   H.M. The King
    Pen and ink on vellum; 30 × 21 (11¾ × 8¼).
    Collections: Richard Mead.
    Said to depict the dress in which the Queen gave thanks for the defeat of the Armada in 1588, but the drawing in fact would appear to be later. Engraved by Crispin Van de Passe, the Elder. The sceptre held in the left hand proves that the drawing was done for an engraving.

8*a.* ISAAC OLIVER.
    WOMAN LEANING ON A PEDESTAL.   Oxford, Ashmolean Museum.
    Pen and bistre and grey wash; 9·5 × 7 (3¾ × 2¾).
    Collections: E. B. (Lugt 827, a collector's mark, which also appears on the drawing of a *Young Boy* by Oliver (Pl.9), and on an Oliver in the former Phillips Fenwick Coll., but otherwise unknown). Lawrence, Thane, Charles Greville, Heseltine. Five similar studies, on one mount, of men and women belong to Sir Robert Witt (ex Coll. Pembroke, Barclay and Clarke).

8*b.* ISAAC OLIVER.
    MOSES STRIKING THE ROCK.   H.M. The King.
    Pen and ink and wash heightened with white; 21 × 33 (8¼ × 13). Signed *Isac: Olivier Fec.* (the signature seems to have been cut out and then reinserted).
    Collections: James II (No. 636 in his Catalogue).
    Lit. Cundall, *Connoisseur,* XCI (1933), p. 356.
    This drawing shows the mixture of influences in Oliver's work, and strongly reflects the style of Paul Moreelse as well as of Parmigianino.

9. ISAAC OLIVER.
    AN UNKNOWN YOUTH.   The Duke of Buccleuch, K.T.
    Pencil and coloured chalk; 19 × 15 (7½ × 5¾).
    Collection: E. B. (see note to Plate 8*a*).
    Often called in the past 'Henry Prince of Wales'. This is unlikely, both on facial resemblance to known portraits and by the fact that he was not born till 1594. The ruff is *c.* 1590.

10. ISAAC OLIVER.
    NYMPHS AND SATYRS—MYTHOLOGICAL DESIGN.   H.M. The King.
    Pen and ink and wash heightened with white; 20·5 × 35·5 (8 × 13¾). Signed *Ollivier.*
    Lit. Cundall, *Connoisseur,* XCI (1933), p. 356.

11. ISAAC OLIVER.
    THE BURIAL OF CHRIST.   British Museum.
    Pen and wash and black chalk; signed *Isa: Ollivier.* 29 × 53 (11¼ × 20¾).
    Collections: Russel, Vertue, Thomas Hollis.
    Lit. Reynolds: *op. cit.,* p. 46.
    Preliminary drawing for a limning, once in the collections of Charles I and James II, now lost. There is a note in the handwriting of George Vertue on the reverse.

12. ISAAC OLIVER.
TWO STUDIES FOR A JUDITH WITH THE HEAD OF HOLOFERNES.
Oxford, Ashmolean Museum.
Pen and bistre; 14×22 (5½×8½). Two further sketches same subject on reverse.
Collection: R. Johnson (Lugt 2216); Randall Davies.

13. PETER OLIVER, B. 1594, D. 1647.
PALLAS ATHENE.
Oxford, Ashmolean Museum.
Pen and bistre with grey wash, over preliminary indications in red chalk. Inscribed *Peter Oliver*.
13·5×15·5 (5¼×6).

14. INIGO JONES, B. 1573, D. 1652.
TWO HEADS FOR 'SALMACIDA SPOLIA'.
Chatsworth Estates Company.
Pen and black ink; 28×18·5 (11×7¼).
Collection: Burlington, Devonshire.
Lit. Simpson and Bell, *Walpole Society,* vol. XII (No. 326).
These are the head of a Fury and a young man in a twisted turban, for Davenant's *Salmacida Spolia*
performed in 1640.

15. INIGO JONES.
IRIS, FOR 'HYMENAEI'.
Chatsworth Estates Company.
Pen and ink and water-colours; 28×19 (11×7½).
Collection: Burlington, Devonshire.
Probably a sketch for the costume of Iris in Ben Jonson's 'Hymenaei'. 1606.
Lit. Simpson and Bell, *Walpole Society,* vol. XII (No. 7).

16. INIGO JONES.
DESIGN FOR 'THE TEMPLE OF LOVE'.
Chatsworth Estates Company.
Pen and brown ink washed with grey; 35·8×35 (14×13¾).
Collections: Burlington, Devonshire.
Connected with Davenant's 'Temple of Love', 1635, Secne III.
Lit. Simpson and Bell, *Walpole Society,* vol. XII (No. 234).

17. INIGO JONES.
NIGHT SCENE FROM 'LUMINALIA'.
Chatsworth Estates Company.
Pen and ink and wash; 17×20 (6¾×7¾).
Collections: Burlington, Devonshire.
Lit. Simpson and Bell, *Walpole Society,* vol. XII (No. 309).
'Luminalia' or the Festival of Light was written by Sir Robert Davenant in 1638. This drawing is
for the background of 'The first sceane of night', and is splashed with scene painter's distemper.

18. UNKNOWN ARTIST, PERHAPS BY ISAAC FULLER, B. 1606. D. 1672.
PORTRAIT OF A MAN.
Mr R. Brinsley Ford.
Black chalk, heightened with white on grey paper. Inscribed '*Vandyck*' by a later hand. 45×33
(17¾×13).

19. UNKNOWN ARTIST. FROM A PAINTING BY VAN DYCK.

GEORGE STUART, LORD D'AUBIGNY. (Killed in 1642 at Edgehill).

Victoria and Albert Museum.

Black chalk heightened with white on blue paper; 36× 24 (14× 9½). Inscribed 'Sir Philip Sidney in the character of ye author of ye Arcadia.'

Collections: Jonathan Richardson, Dyce.

The painting by Van Dyck is in the collection of the Earl of Darnley, Cobham Hall, Kent. It appeared at Christie's 1. v. 1925 (lot 85), and is reproduced in the Catalogue. Mr Waterhouse has suggested that it might be by Lely, in which case this drawing could be an early example of that artist essaying a Van Dyck pose.

20. ROBERT WALKER, B. c. 1610. D. 1658.

LADY BEAUCHAMP, LATER DUCHESS OF BEAUFORT (1630–1714/15).

The Duke of Beaufort, K.G.

Red chalk; 26× 21 (10¼× 8¼).

Drawing for the painting by Robert Walker at Badminton, which shows her as a widow (1654–1657), three-quarter length, standing, in black.

21. ISAAC FULLER, B. 1606. D. 1672.

SELF PORTRAIT.   Victoria and Albert Museum.

Pen and ink; 21× 17 (8¼× 6¾).

Collection: Dyce.

This seems to be a study for the head in his well known *Self Portrait when Drunk* in the Bodleian at Oxford, in which he holds a drawing. There are other versions, without the drawing and with variations, in The Queen's College, Oxford and the National Portrait Gallery.

Engraved by T. Chambars for the 4th edition of Walpole's *Anecdotes of Painting,* 1763, vol. III, p. 4.

22. WILLIAM FAITHORNE, B. 1616. D. 1691.

JOHN AUBREY, (1626–1697).   Oxford, Ashmolean Museum.

Black lead, face touched with red, on vellum; 20× 14.5 (8¾× 5¾). Inscribed 'Mr John Aubrey, R.S.S., 1666, Aetatis 40'. On the back-board of the frame is written in Aubrey's hand: *Effigies Johannis Awbrey de Easton Pierse Guliel: Faythorne Amicitiae ergo adumbravit An Dm 1666.*

Given to the Ashmolean by the sitter.

Lit. Bell, *Walpole Society,* vol. V. p.2.

John Aubrey was himself an amateur painter, and there exists a water-colour by him representing his house.

23. SAMUEL COOPER, B. 1609, D. 1672.

THOMAS ALCOCK.   Oxford, Ashmolean Museum.

Black chalk on buff paper; 18× 11.5 (7× 4½). Inscribed on the back-board of the frame: *This picture was drawne for mee at the Earle of Westmorelands house at Apethorpe, in Northampton-Shire by the greate, (tho' little) limner, the then famous Mr Cooper of Covent Garden: when I was eighteen years of age.* Signed *Thomas Alcock preceptor.*

Bequeathed to the University by Dr Rawlinson in 1755. Transferred to the Ashmolean Museum from the Bodleian, 1897.

Lit. Bell, *Walpole Society,* vol. V. p. 2.

24. WILLIAM FAITHORNE.

PORTRAIT OF A MAN HOLDING A PETITION.   Oxford, Ashmolean Museum.

Pastel; 27× 22. (10½× 8½) Inscribed at the top *Jan: 26 1679. Aetat 36* and at the bottom *W* (with a 'G' superimposed by a later hand) *Faithorne del.*

Attached to the drawing is a label identifying it as a portrait of 'a gentleman of the Dare family'. In the *Domestic State Papers* for 'March 29th 1679/80 Taunton:' 'Petition of the Grand Jury of Somerset at the assizes Disowning the petition lately delivered to his majesty by Thomas Dare of this town goldsmith, in the name of the inhabitants and freeholders of Somerset, for the sitting of the parliament and desiring that Popish Recusants be proceeded against and that the laws against Nonconformists be put in execution'. See also entries for April 1st and April 3rd 1680. This may be the sitter.

25. WILLIAM FAITHORNE.

AN UNKNOWN MAN.   Mr Edward Croft-Murray.

Pastel; 25× 19 (9¾× 7½).

Collection: J. F. Keane, Sotheby's 3. vi. 47 (small lot 157).

26. FRANCIS BARLOW, B. 1626. D. 1702.

THREE SQUIRRELS.   Christ Church, Oxford.

Pen and wash; 18 × 31 (7× 12).

Collection: Guise.

Engraved with variations in 'Various Birds and Beasts', 'I. Griffier fecit, P. Tempest ex.'

27. FRANCIS BARLOW.

HUNTING SCENE.   Oxford, Ashmolean Museum.

Pen and wash; 21 × 31 (8¼× 12¼).

Collections: E. Peart, Douce. Etched by Hollar 1671, Parthey, p. 440, No. 2029 (2).

Lit. Shaw Sparrow, *Connoisseur,* XCVIII, 1936, p. 40.

One of the many drawings of sporting life by Barlow. Among these may be mentioned *Hawking for Pheasants* in the Ashmolean Museum, dated 1684; a *Hawking Scene,* coll. Sir Robert Witt; *Hunting the Hare,* coll. Leonard Duke; *Woodland Scene with Animals,* coll. Sir Edward Marsh.

28. FRANCIS BARLOW.

A GROUP OF BIRDS.   Sir Bruce Ingram.

Pen and wash; 18 × 25·5 (7× 10). Engraved with variations in 'Various Birds and Beasts', 'I. Griffier fecit, E. Cooper, ex.'

The birds include a cassowary, pheasant, ostrich, peacock and peahen.

29. FRANCIS BARLOW.

CAT AND KITTENS.   Sir Robert Witt.

Pen and wash; 13 × 18.5 (5× 7¼). Signed *F. Barlow 1684.*

30. FRANCIS BARLOW.

EAGLE AND HARE.   Sir Robert Witt.

Pen and wash; 13 × 17 (5× 6½). Signed *F. Barlow.*

A variation of this drawing was used for the frontispiece of 'Various Birds and Beasts', 'Francis Place fecit, E. Cooper exud.'

CATALOGUE OF PLATES

31. Francis Barlow.   Sir Robert Witt.
ELEPHANT AND RHINOCEROS.
Pen and wash; 21 × 30 (8¼ × 11¾).
The rhinoceros is taken from Dürer's woodcut (Bartsch 136) of 1515.

32. Francis Barlow.
FOX AND EAGLE   Oxford, Ashmolean Museum.
Pen and wash; 25 × 18·5 (9¾ × 7¼).
Collections: John Thane, Douce.
Lit. Shaw Sparrow, *Connoisseur*, XCVIII, 1936, p. 36.
Engraved for Ogilby's *Aesopico*, 1668.

33a. Wenceslas Hollar, B. 1607, D. 1677.
A LADY'S MUFF.   British Museum.
Brush drawing in indian ink and body colour; 7 × 9·6 (2¾ × 3¾).
Collection: Sloane.
Engraved by the artist, 1647 (Pathey No. 1946).
Lit. K. T. Parker, *Old Master Drawings,* vol. VI, Sept., 1931, p. 38.

33b. Richard Gaywood (w. about 1650–80).
'MUSICK'S DELIGHT ON THE CITHERN'.   British Museum.
Indian ink and wash; 8 × 13 (3 × 5).
Design engraved for Playford's book of that name, 1666.

34. Sir Peter Lely, B. 1618. D. 1680.
THE CHANCELLOR OF THE ORDER OF THE GARTER.
                               Amsterdam, Rijksprentenkabinet.
Black and coloured chalks; 50 × 30 (19¾ × 11¾). Inscribed 'P. Lely and de Cancelier der Ordre Van | de Kousebond met een | Violet fluweele Mantel'.
Collections: Ploos Van Amstel, Jac. de Vos Jacsz.

This drawing and Plates 35, 36, and 37 belong to a series of drawings of the principal officers of the Knights of the Garter. Some of these are first mentioned in an anonymous sale organized by de Leth in Amsterdam 23rd March 1763, purchased by Johan Vandenmarck. There were then 16 numbered drawings by Lely in a 'Teekeningen Konstboeck'. After Vandenmarck's death in 1773 they were sold separately. See Michel Benisovich, *Two Drawings by Peter Lely, Burlington Magazine*, vol. XCI (1949) p. 79 and *Burlington Magazine,* vol. LIII (1928) p. 61–7 and p. 208. They are now distributed, as far as is known, as follows: ten in the British Museum, one in the Albertina, two at Amsterdam, and one to each of the following: The Hermitage, Sir Robert Witt, The Hague (de Stuers Collection), Ashmolean (Sutherland Collection, Burnett II, 722), Chatsworth, Mr Frits Lugt, C. P. Van Eeghen, Fogg Museum, Crocker Art Gallery (Sacramento), and a slight one in the Ashmolean. One or two have appeared on the market in recent years.

35. Sir Peter Lely.
STUDY OF TWO HERALDS.   Sir Robert Witt.
Black chalk on grey paper; 50·8 × 36·2 (20 × 14½).

D

36. Sir Peter Lely.

THE PRELATE OF THE ORDER OF THE GARTER.   British Museum.

Black chalk heightened with white on blue paper; 51 × 37 (20× 14½). Inscribed 'The (?) Prelate of the Order',

This is probably George Morley, Bishop of Winchester (1597–1684), who wore a beard. A portrait of him late in life, clad in Garter robes, can be seen in the National Portrait Gallery.

37. Sir Peter Lely.

A KNIGHT OF THE GARTER   Chatsworth Estates Company.

Black chalk heightened with white on blue paper; 46·8 × 37·3 (18½ × 14¾).
Collection: Warwick (Christie's 1896).

38. Sir Peter Lely.

SELF PORTRAIT.   Mrs H. M. Lely.

Black chalk heightened with white; 36× 28 (14¼ × 11). Signed *P. Lely fecit.*

39. Sir Peter Lely.

A YOUNG GIRL.   The Lady Islington.

Black chalk heightened with white; 28 × 17 (11 × 6¾). Signed P. Lely.
Collection: Sir Joshua Reynolds.

Apart from those reproduced in this book there are other excellent female portraits by Lely at Windsor, in the collection of Sir Robert Witt, the National Gallery of Scotland, and the Pierpont Morgan Library.

40. Sir Peter Lely.

PORTRAIT OF A WOMAN, WEARING A HOOD.   British Museum.

Chalks on brown paper; 24× 18 (9½× 7¼). Signed P. Lely.

Wrongly called Barbara, Duchess of Cleveland, to whose features it bears no resemblance. No drawing of her by Lely has yet been identified.

41. Sir Peter Lely.

PORTRAIT OF A WOMAN.   British Museum.

Chalks on brown paper; 24× 18·5 (9½× 7¼).
Collections: Lord Spencer, Esdaile.

42. Sir Peter Lely.

STUDIES OF HANDS.   Oxford, Ashmolean Museum.

Red, black and white chalks on brown paper; 38× 26·8 (15× 10½).
Collections: Sir P. Lely, T. Hudson, Marignane.

The upper hand and the one holding the staff are for his portrait of the *Countess of Falmouth*; the other for *Frances Stewart, Duchess of Richmond*, both in the *Windsor Beauties* series at Hampton Court.

43. Sir Peter Lely.

STUDIES OF HANDS.   Cambridge, Fitzwilliam Museum.

Black chalk heightened with white; 19·4× 27·5 (7½× 10¾).
Collection: Ricketts and Shannon.

CATALOGUE OF PLATES

These hands are for the portrait called *Jane Middleton* by Lely in the Pitti Palace at Florence (at one time on loan to the Italian Embassy in London). In the painting the pearls are replaced by a chain.

44. SIR PETER LELY.
    PORTRAIT OF A MAN IN A TURBAN.   Victoria and Albert Museum.
Black and red chalk; 40× 35 (15¾× 13¾). Signed *P. L.* in monogram.
Collection: Sir P. Lely.

45. SIR PETER LELY.
    LADY AS A SHEPHERDESS.   Oxford, Ashmolean Museum.
Black, white, and red chalk on buff paper; 25·4× 19·1 (10× 7½).
Collections: F. C. Lewis, Rev. R. Finch.
Sometimes wrongly identified as Lady Castlemaine.
Lit.: Bell, *Walpole Society,* vol. V. p. 8.

46. SIR PETER LELY.
    SUSANNAH AND THE ELDERS.   Sir Robert Witt.
Black chalk on buff paper; 18·5× 25 (7¼× 9¾).
Collections: R. Udney, C. Fairfax Murray, Victor Koch. Sotheby's, 29 June 1949 (lot 86).
    This composition corresponds with the picture formerly in the L.W. Neeld and Lord Gwydir Collections, sold Sotheby's, 23 March 1949 (lot 138). I am informed by Mr Oliver Millar that a bill also exists for this painting. Other versions of this painting, with alterations in design, are at Birmingham and in the collection of the Marquis of Exeter.
    This is the only known subject drawing by Lely. Others are attributed to Lely in various public and private collections, but would seem dubious, excepting perhaps a study, presumably for an *Europa*, at Oxford, which has good claims to be rightly attributed.

47. ATTRIBUTED TO PROSPER HENRY LANKRINK, B. 1628, D. 1692.
    A LADY AT A FOUNTAIN.   Oxford, Ashmolean Museum.
Pen and bistre; 41× 27 (16× 10½).
Collections: Lankrink; Randall Davies.
Lit. Randall Davies, *Chats on Old Master Drawings* (repr.); Binyon, *Burlington Magazine,* vol. X, p. 74 (repr.)
    This drawing, formerly ascribed to Lely, is here tentatively given to Lankrink on the slender grounds of the Smith mezzotint of *Nymphs Bathing* in the British Museum.

48. SIR PETER LELY.
    JOHN GREENHILL.   British Museum.
Pastel on grey paper; 27·5× 20·5 (10¾× 8).
Collections: Richardson, J. C. Robinson.
For a discussion on Greenhill's Portraits see Waterhouse, *Old Master Drawings,* vol. XI, 1937, No. 44, p. 69.

49. JOHN GREENHILL, B. 1649. D. 1676.

SELF PORTRAIT. British Museum.

Black and red chalk on drab paper, heightened with white; 23·8 × 19·4 (9½ × 7¾). Signed *J. G.* in monogram.

Lit. Waterhouse, *Old Master Drawings*, vol. XI, 1937, No. 44, p. 69.

There is another *Self Portrait* in oils at Dulwich, reproduced in C. H. Collins Baker's *Lely and the Stuart Portrait Painters*, Pl. II, facing p. 6.

50. SIR PETER LELY.

PORTRAIT OF A WOMAN. Amsterdam, Rijksprentenkabinet.

Black, red, and white chalks on light brown paper; 26·5 × 20 (10½ × 7¾). Signed and dated 1658. Collection: Bellingham Smith.

Lit. Binyon, *Old Master Drawings*, II, June 1927, p. 14. (repr.). Dated drawings by Lely are rare: but there is a further one, also dated 1658, in the Morgan Library (Coll. Fairfax Murray).

51. JOHN GREENHILL.

PORTRAIT OF JOSEPH HARRIS AS CARDINAL WOLSEY.

Oxford, Magdalen College (President's Lodgings).

Coloured chalks on buff paper; 31 × 41 (12¼ × 16). Signed *J. G. del 1664*. Engraved by Place.

Collection: Provenance unknown, but was at Magdalen during the Presidency of Dr Routh (1755–1854), as it appears in a water-colour of his study by J. B. Pyne in the Ashmolean Museum (another version at Magdalen College).

Vertue noticed: 'at the Lord Halifax at Westminster . . . Mr Harris a player afterwards Mint Graver, by Greenhill.'

There is another, less finished and more rubbed version in the Ashmolean, probably also by Greenhill. Horace Walpole owned a painting, now at the Garrick Club, which is a copy from the engraving. The Magdalen and Kingston Lacy drawings (Pl. 53), together with the Cartwright portraits at Dulwich, prove that Greenhill was associated with actors earlier than has usually been assumed. These are also the two earliest known portraits of English actors in costume.

52. T. THRUMTON (OR THRUMPTON), Active 1662–1673.

PORTRAIT OF A YOUNG MAN. Oxford, Ashmolean Museum.

Black chalk and pastel on buff paper; 23·5 × 19 (9¼ × 7½). Signed T. Thrumpton feci Londini 1662.

Collection: Douce.

Lit. Bell, *Walpole Society*, vol. V, 1917, pp. 6–8.

On the reverse, reproduced by Bell, is a portrait of *Mary Carleton* inscribed '*Ye Jarman Princes*'.

There is a further drawing signed 'Thrumpton ye 16 . 7' in the collection of Mr J. Isaacs. The Ashmolean also owns a drawing of an *Unknown Man*, which may be by the same hand, though it is coarser in handling.

53. JOHN GREENHILL.

PORTRAIT OF THOMAS BETTERTON AS BAJAZET.

Mr. H. J. R. Bankes.

Coloured chalks on buff paper; 47 × 36 (18¾ × 14¼). Signed *J. G. del 1663*.

This drawing has previously been attributed to Sir Peter Lely and to Edmund Lilley. Mr Oliver Millar first noticed the signature and brought it to my notice. Vertue notices that 'Mr. Bullfinch bought all Mr. Betterton's Pictures amongst which were a great many Crayon pictures of famous Playereses these he sold to Mr. Sykes'.

54*a*. DAVID LOGGAN, B. 1635, D. about 1700.

JOHN WILMOT, EARL OF ROCHESTER. (Identity not certain.)   British Museum.

Plumbago, face tinted, on vellum; oval 13·7 × 11·6 ($5\frac{1}{2}$ × $4\frac{1}{2}$). Signed *D. L. delin 1671*.

Plumbago heads by Loggan are numerous, but this is one of the few finished with such minute exactness and tinted. For reproductions of other work by plumbago artists see C. F. Bell, *Walpole Society*, vol. XIV.

54*b*. FRANCIS PLACE, B. 1647. D. 1728.

A BRIDGE.   H.M. The King.

Pen and wash; 6 × 35 ($2\frac{1}{2}$ × $13\frac{3}{4}$).

55. MARY BEALE, B. 1632, D. 1699.

PAGE FROM A SKETCH BOOK.   Victoria and Albert Museum.

Chalk, pen and ink, and wash; 27 × 21 ($10\frac{1}{2}$ × $8\frac{1}{4}$).

Collection: Bernard Webb.

This page, from a sketch book containing some 48 ff. of drawings, shows a study of an unidentified man, his hands, and figures for a *Judgment of Paris*. The sketch book contains copies of recognisable works of Van Dyck and Lely (including a portrait of the latter, seated at his easel and holding brushes and palette, on ff 23) and what could be a copy of Rembrandt's *Polish Officer*. There can be no question that these drawings are by Mary Beale, though a few drawings of extremely poor quality, probably by her son, have been inserted.

56. FRANCIS PLACE.

MAN FISHING.   Sir Bruce Ingram.

Pen and wash; 12 × 20 ($4\frac{3}{4}$ × $7\frac{3}{4}$). Inscribed *Richmond Foss*

57. FRANCIS PLACE.

VIEW OF THE HAGUE.   Sir Bruce Ingram.

Pen and sepia wash; 12·5 × 20·5 (5 × 8).

58. EDWARD GIBSON, B. 1668, D. 1701.

SELF PORTRAIT.   National Portrait Gallery.

Coloured chalk; 26·8 × 19 ($10\frac{1}{2}$ × $7\frac{1}{2}$). Signed *E. Gibson fecit 1690*.

Collections: Lawrence, Thane, Bulwers of East Dereham, F. Wellesley.

Vertue saw in Thomas Gibson's Collection in 1713 two self portraits, 'one dress'd as a chinese another like a quaker with a hat on'. He saw another 'of 1690' some thirty years later in Lord Stafford's Collection. It is not certain which, if any, of these this may be. No other is known.

59. EDWARD LUTTEREL, B. *c.* 1650. D. after 1723.
    KING CHARLES II.   Mr Leonard Duke.
    Pastel on buff paper; 24·5 × 18 (9½ × 7).
    Collection: Col. Fernyhough.
    There is a very similar portrait of James II, when Duke of York, in the collection of Sir Bruce
Ingram.

60. EDMUND ASHFIELD. Worked from *c.* 1675–*c.* 1700.
    PORTRAIT OF A GENTLEMAN.   Mr W. Plowden.
    Pastel and body-colour; 29·5 × 24·5 (11½ × 9¾). Signed and dated *E. A. 1676.*
    There is an article on Ashfield by Collins Baker, *Walpole Society,* vol. III.

61. SIR GODFREY KNELLER, BT.: B. 1646/49, D. 1723.
    PORTRAIT OF A GENTLEMAN.   Sir Bruce Ingram.
    Black chalk on blue paper, heightened with white; 36·5 × 29·5 (14¼ × 11¾). Inscribed *Sir Godfrey
Kneller origin.*
    It should not be hard to identify this head, but careful scrutiny of photographs of Kneller's portraits
has so far been negative. The puzzling inscription, which appears to read 'P. L. (in monogram) 44', has
not been explained. It is remarkably like the usual signature of Lely, to whom the drawing cannot be
given, and may be an inventory number perhaps from a studio record book.

62. SIR GODFREY KNELLER, BT.
    HEAD OF A YOUNG MAN.   Sir Robert Witt.
    Black chalk, heightened with white, on brown paper; 35 × 28 (13¾ × 11). Inscribed *Sir Godfrey
Kneller 1712.*
    This drawing though similar to several others by Kneller, is of such high quality that its authorship
is not entirely without question. Alan Ramsay, to whose youthful self portraits it bears a distinct resemblance, may in fact be the artist.

63. JOHN VANDERBANK, B. *c.* 1694. D. 1739.
    STUDY OF A HAND.   Sir Robert Witt.
    Black chalk heightened with white; 39 × 25.5 (15¼ × 10). Signed *J. V.* in monogram.
    The portrait for which this is a study has not been recognized.

64. SIR GODFREY KNELLER, BT.
    A DEER.   British Museum.
    Chalks on drab paper; 32 × 25·2 (12½ × 10).
    A study for the deer in the portrait of *Lord Buckhurst and Lady Mary Sackville* at Knole. Other animal
drawings by Kneller are in the British Museum: *A Greyhound;* and studies of *Horses* for the background
of a portrait of *Lt.-Gen. George Ramsay of Cariden* in the collection of the Earl of Dalhousie.

INDEX OF PERSONS

Alençon, duc de, 15
Anne of Denmark, Queen, 19, 20
Arundel, Thomas Earl of, 12, 13, 14, 17, 19, 23, 29, 31, 43, 44
Ashfield, Edmund, 27, 35, 38, 54
Aubrey, John, 38, 47

Bacon, Sir Nathaniel, 28
Barlow, Francis, 20, 22, 24, 25, 48, 49
Beale, Charles, 33, 35
Beale, Charles, the Younger, 33, 36, 38
Beale, Mary, 27, 36, 37, 53
Bernini, Lorenzo, 21, 40
Bossam, John, 15
Brill, Paul, 19
Brownover, Sylvester, 38
Bry, Dirk de, 17
Buckeridge, B., 25
Buckingham, George Villiers duke of, 17
Busby, Richard, 35

Caroline, Queen, 12, 43, 44
Cartwright, William, 36
Catherine de Medici, 16
Chamberlaine, John, 43, 44
Champaigne, Philip de, 17
Charles I, 17, 19, 20, 28, 29, 30, 31
Charles II, 31, 33, 43
Cleveland, Barbara, duchess of, 27, 33
Cleyn, Francis, 22, 29, 49
Cleyn, Francis, the Younger, 22
Cleyn, John, 22
Clouet, François, 15
Cooper, Samuel, 27, 30, 33, 38, 47

Dahl, Michael, 35
Davenant, Sir William, 21, 46
Devonshire, William, 2nd duke of, 37
Devonshire, William, 3rd duke of, 37
Dobson, William, 17, 21, 29, 30, 40
Dryden, John, 34
Dumonstiers, Daniel, 27
Dunstall, John, 26
Dürer, Albert, 15
Dyck, Anthonie Van, 13, 17, 21, 23, 28, 29, 30, 31, 34, 37, 47

Edward VI, 12
Elizabeth, Queen, 14, 15, 16, 20
Elizabeth of York, Queen, 43

Elsheimer, Adam, 19, 21
Evelyn, John, 26
Eworth, Hans, 14

Faber, John, 28
Faithorne, William, 27, 30, 35, 47, 48
Fisher, Bishop John, 43, 44
Flatman, Thomas, 37
Forster, Thomas, 28
Francis I, 16
Fruytiers, Philip de, 13
Fuller, Isaac, 29, 30, 35, 46, 47
Fuller, Isaac, the Younger, 29

Gainsborough, Thomas, 25, 40
Gaywood, Richard, 22, 23, 49
Gerbier, Sir Balthasar, 29
Gibson, Edward, 37, 53
Gibson, Richard, 36, 37
Gibson, Thomas, 36, 53
Gibson, William, 36, 37
Golztius, Hendrik, 18
Greenhill, John, 27, 35, 36, 40, 51, 52
Guercino, 21, 40
Gyles, Henry, 24

Haeken, Joseph Van, 28
Haydocke, Richard, 15
Henrietta Maria, Queen, 20
Henry VII, 11, 43
Henry VIII, 12, 13, 43
Henry, Prince of Wales, 17, 45
Here, Lucas de, 14
Hilliard, Nicholas, 12, 14, 15, 16, 18, 19, 29, 44
Hoefnagel, Joris, 14
Holbein, Hans, the Younger, 11, 12, 13, 14, 16, 32, 33, 43
Hollar, Wenceslas, 23, 24, 25, 34, 49
Hoskins, John, 29
Hudson, Thomas 32, 35
Huygens, Constantin, 32
Huysmans, Jacob, 35

Isabella, Archduchess, 17

James I, 15, 17, 20, 28
Jane Seymour, Queen, 43
Johnson, Cornelius, 28
Johnson, Thomas, 25
Jones, Inigo, 18, 19, 20, 21, 46
Jonson, Ben, 20

INDEX OF PERSONS

Killigrew, Anne, 34
Kneller, Sir Godfrey, 28, 30, 39, 40, 54

Lambert, John, 24
Landseer, Sir Edwin, 25
Lanier, Nicholas, 32
Lankrink, Prosper Henry, 32, 34, 51
Lawrence, Sir Thomas, 32
Leemput, Regius Van, 43
Leicester, Robert Dudley, Earl of, 14
Lely, Sir Peter, 27–54
Lodge, William, 24, 25
Loggan, David, 28, 38, 53
Louis XIII, 17
Lutteral, Edward, 27, 35, 38, 54

Manby, Thomas, 26
Mander, Carel Van, 14
Maratta, Carlo, 40
Marmion, Sir Edmund, 23
Mary I, 14
Mary II, 32, 36
Mellan, Claude, 27
Montagu, Lady Mary Wortley, 31, 39
Moreelse, Paul, 18, 45
Mytens, Daniel, 17, 28

Nanteuil, Robert, 27
Norden, John, 17
Norgate, Edward, 13
North, Roger, 31, 32

Oliver, Isaac, 14, 15, 18, 19, 20, 45, 46
Oliver, Peter, 20, 46

Palladio, Andrea, 21
Parigi, Alfonso, 21
Parigi, Giulio, 21
Parmigianino, 18, 19, 45
Peachum, Henry, 26
Peake, Robert, 29
Pepys, Samuel, 27
Philip II, of Spain, 14
Philip IV, of Spain, 17

Place, Francis, 24, 25, 26, 53
Polidoro Caldara, 36
Pope, Alexander, 31, 39

Ramsay, Alan, 39, 54
Rembrandt Van Rijn, 17, 40
Reynolds, Sir Joshua, 32, 35, 40
Richardson, Jonathan, the Elder, 32, 35, 37, 40
Richardson, Jonathan, the Younger, 37
Riley, John, 35, 40
Rottenhammer, Johann, 19
Rubens, Peter Paul, 17, 23, 37

Simon, Thomas, 30
Soest, Gerard, 35
Somer, Paul Van, 17, 28
Surrey, Henry Howard Earl of, 12, 43

Teniers, David, the Younger, 20
Thomas, John, 17
Thornhill, Sir James, 21, 40
Thoresby, Ralph, 24, 27
Thrumpton, T., 37, 52
Tilson, Henry, 35

Vandendoort, Abraham, 19, 28
Vanderbank, John, 40, 54
Verrio, Antonio, 34
Vertue, George, 12, 18, 20, 22, 32, 35, 43, 44, 45, 52, 53
Volpe, Vincent, 17

Walpole, Horace, 39, 52
Walker, Robert, 17, 30, 40, 47
Webb, John, 18
West, Benjamin, 32
White, John, 16
White, Robert, 28
Wissing, William, 35
Wren, Sir Christopher, 18
Wright, John Michael, 33, 35, 38
Wyngaerde, A. Van den, 14

Zuccaro, Federico, 14, 16

INDEX OF COLLECTIONS

Agnew, Messrs. Thomas, 44
Amsterdam, Rijksprentenkabinet, 49, 52

Banks, H. J. R., Kingston Lacy, 36, 52
Beaufort, Duke of, 30, 47
Birmingham, Barber Institute, 23
Buccleuch, Duke of, 19, 45

Cambridge, Fitzwillizm Museum, 19, 33, 49
Chatsworth Estates Company, 11, 12, 20, 21, 23, 43,
   46, 52
Christ Church, Oxford, 48
Clarke, Louis, 15
Croft-Murray, Edward, 48

Dublin, National Gallery, 38
Duke, L. G., 33, 38, 48, 54
Dulwich Gallery, 36, 52

Edinburgh, National Gallery, 28, 40

Ford, Brinsley, 29, 46

Grant, Lady Sybil, 38

Ham House, Richmond, 38
Hampton Court, 43

Ingram, Sir Bruce, 24, 35, 38, 44, 48, 53, 54
Isaacs, J., 52
Islington, The Lady, 50

Lely, Mrs. H. M., 33, 50
London, British Museum, 14, 16, 21-4, 26, 29, 33, 35,
   36, 40, 44, 45, 49-54
London, National Portrait Gallery, 13, 38, 44, 53
London, Victoria and Albert Museum, 13, 19, 29, 30,
   33, 35, 37, 44, 47, 51, 53

Magdalen College, Oxford, 36, 52
Malcolm, Sir Neil, 33
Marsh, Sir Edward, 48
Munich, Graphische Sammlung, 13, 33, 43

New York, Morgan Library, 12, 44
Northumberland, the Duke of, 29, 31

Oppé, A. P., 24, 35
Oxford, Ashmolean Museum, 21, 22, 30, 33-7, 45-52
Oxford, Bodleian Library, 29, 37, 47

Plowden, W., 38, 54

Rotterdam, Boymans Museum, 13
Rutland, Duke of, 34

Spencer, The Earl, 29
St. Germans, The Earl of, 36

Trinity College, Cambridge, 39

Wadham College, Oxford, 22
Windsor Castle, Royal Library, 11, 12, 19, 30, 33, 40,
   44, 45, 53
Witt, Sir Robert, 29, 33, 39, 48, 49, 51, 54

PLATES

1. Unknown Artist, after Hans Holbein: Henry VIII

Munich

2. UNKNOWN ARTIST: Henry Howard, Earl of Surrey
Reproduced by Gracious Permission of H.M. The King

3. UNKNOWN ARTIST: Henry Howard, Earl of Surrey
Morgan Library

4. UNKNOWN ARTIST: Bishop John Fisher
National Portrait Gallery

5. NICHOLAS HILLIARD: Design for Queen Elizabeth's
Great Seal of Ireland

British Museum

6. NICHOLAS HILLIARD: A Lady in Court Dress
Victoria and Albert Museum

7. ISAAC OLIVER: Queen Elizabeth

Reproduced by Gracious Permission of H.M. The King

8a. ISAAC OLIVER: A Lady leaning on a Pedestal
Ashmolean Museum

8b. ISAAC OLIVER: Moses Striking the Rock
Reproduced by Gracious Permission of H.M. The King

9. Isaac Oliver: Unknown Youth

The Duke of Buccleuch, K.T.

10. ISAAC OLIVER: Nymphs and Satyrs

Reproduced by Gracious Permission of H.M. The King

11. ISAAC OLIVER: The Burial of Christ

British Museum

12. ISAAC OLIVER: Two Studies for a Judith with the head of Holofernes
Ashmolean Museum

13. Peter Oliver: Pallas Athene
Ashmolean Museum

14. Inigo Jones: Two Heads for *Salmacida Spolia*
Copyright Chatsworth Estates Company

15. INIGO JONES: Iris
Copyright Chatsworth Estates Company

16. INIGO JONES: Design for *The Temple of Love*

17. INIGO JONES: Night Scene from '*Luminalia*'
Copyright Chatsworth Estates Company

18. ATTRIBUTED TO ISAAC FULLER: Portrait of a Man

Mr. R. Brinsley Ford

19. UNKNOWN ARTIST, AFTER VAN DYCK: George Stuart,
Lord D'Aubigny

Victoria and Albert Museum

20. ROBERT WALKER: Lady Beauchamp.
The Duke of Beaufort, K.G.

21. ISAAC FULLER: Self Portrait.
Victoria and Albert Museum

22. WILLIAM FAITHORNE: John Aubrey
Ashmolean Museum

23. SAMUEL COOPER: Thomas Alcock
Ashmolean Museum

Jan: 26. 1679.   Ætat: 36

W. Faithorne dele

24. WILLIAM FAITHORNE: Portrait of a Man
Ashmolean Museum

25. WILLIAM FAITHORNE: Portrait of a Man

Mr. Edward Croft-Murray

26. Francis Barlow: Squirrels
Christ Church, Oxford

27. FRANCIS BARLOW: Hunting Scene
Ashmolean Museum

28. FRANCIS BARLOW: A Group of Birds
Sir Bruce Ingram

29. FRANCIS BARLOW: Cat and Kittens

Sir Robert Witt

30. Francis Barlow: Eagle and Hare

Sir Robert Witt

31. FRANCIS BARLOW: Elephant and Rhinoceros
Sir Robert Witt

32. FRANCIS BARLOW: The Fox and the Eagle
Ashmolean Museum

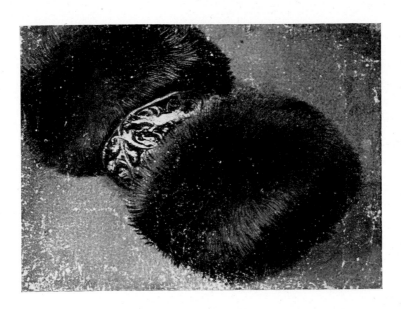

33a. WENCESLAS HOLLAR: A Lady's Muff

British Museum

33b. RICHARD GAYWOOD: *'Musick's Delight on the Cithern'*

British Museum

34. Sir Peter Lely: The Chancellor of the Order of the Garter

rijksprentenkabinet, Amsterdam

35. SIR PETER LELY: Two Heralds

Sir Robert Witt

36. SIR PETER LELY: The Prelate of the Order of the Garter
British Museum

37. Sir Peter Lely: A Knight of the Garter
Copyright Chatsworth Estates Company

38. SIR PETER LELY: Self-Portrait

Mrs H. M. Lely

39. Sir Peter Lely: A Young Girl

The Lady Islington

40. SIR PETER LELY: Portrait of a Woman
British Museum

41. SIR PETER LELY: Portrait of a Woman
British Museum

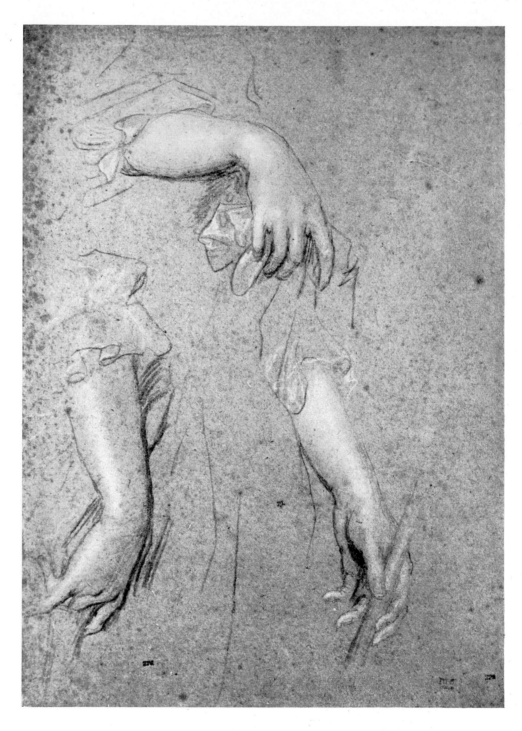

42. SIR PETER LELY: Studies of Hands
Ashmolean Museum

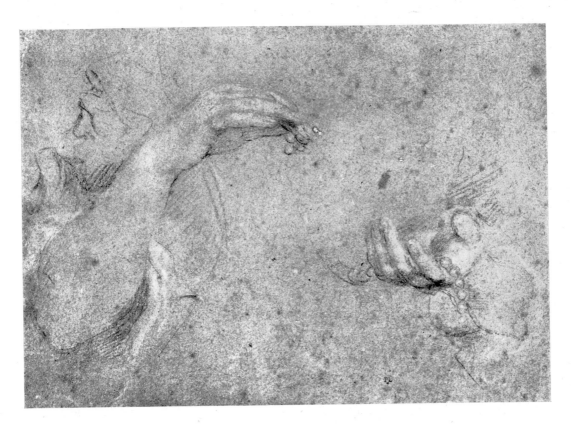

43. SIR PETER LELY: Studies of Hands
Fitzwilliam Museum

44. SIR PETER LELY: Portrait of a Man
Victoria and Albert Museum

45. SIR PETER LELY: A Lady as a Shepherdess
Ashmolean Museum

46. SIR PETER LELY: Susannah and the Elders

Sir Robert Witt

47. ATTRIBUTED TO P. H. LANKRINK: Lady at a Fountain
Ashmolean Museum

48. SIR PETER LELY: John Greenhill
British Museum

49. JOHN GREENHILL: Self-Portrait
British Museum

50. Sir Peter Lely: Portrait of a Woman

rijksprentenkabinet, Amsterdam

51. JOHN GREENHILL: Portrait of Joseph Harris as Cardinal Wolsey
Magdalen College, Oxford

52. T. THRUMTON (OR THRUMPTON): Portrait of a Young Man
Ashmolean Musueum

53. JOHN GREENHILL: Portrait of Thomas Betterton as Bajazet
Mr. H. J. R. Banks

54a. DAVID LOGGAN: The Earl of Rochester
British Museum

54b. FRANCIS PLACE: A Bridge
Reproduced by Gracious Permission of H.M. The King

55. MARY BEALE: Page from her Sketch-book

Victoria and Albert Museum

56. FRANCIS PLACE: A Man Fishing
Sir Bruce Ingram

57. FRANCIS PLACE: View of the Hague
Sir Bruce Ingram

58. EDWARD GIBSON: Self-Portrait
National Portrait Gallery

59. Edward Lutteral: Charles II

Mr. L. G. Duke

60. EDMUND ASHFIELD: Portrait of a Man
Mr. W. Plowden

61. Sir Godfrey Kneller: Portrait of a Gentleman

Sir Bruce Ingram

62. SIR GODFREY KNELLER: Head of a Young Man
Sir Robert Witt

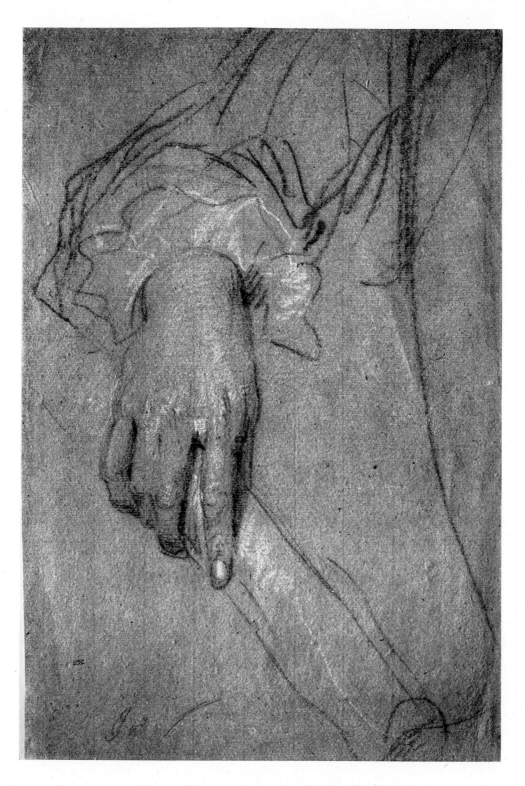

63. JOHN VANDERBANK: Study of a Hand
Sir Robert Witt

64. SIR GODFREY KNELLER: Study of a Deer
British Museum